OTHER BOOKS BY JOHN D. FREEMAN

Rockport: A Childhood by the Sea
Freedom, Tribalism and Creativity: A Challenge to our Syrian Friends
A Politically Incorrect Guide to Health Care Reform

JUNGLE EPISODES
A Missionary Doctor in Thailand

By John D. Freeman, M.D.

JUNGLE EPISODES: A MISSIONARY DOCTOR IN THAILAND
By: John D. Freeman, M.D.

All rights reserved. Except for brief exerpts for review purposes, no part of this book may be reproduced or used in any form without written permission from the author.

ISBN-13: 978-1492776338
ISBN-10: 1492776335

© 2013 John D. Freeman
All Rights Reserved.

Editorial assistance was provided by Dr. Louise Bently
Cover and Layout Design: Kate Weekes
Cover Images and Book Images: John D. Freeman

Printed in the United States of America

Front cover image - This scene was encountered on our way to a village clinic. The elephants belong to General Lee and are pulling sledges loaded with wolfram ore (tungsten) headed toward Bangkok.

PREFACE

During the years that we spent in Thailand as medical missionaries we had some interesting experiences that occurred in several different places where we worked. These were all in rural areas so the experiences reflect life in rural areas and jungle places beginning with the early seventies. This is a compilation of documents written at different times to give a picture of the life of a jungle doctor.

The story of how God led me to that part of the world to do that kind of work is one that I hope will be an inspiration to my grandchildren and of course others who may read it. A person with meager academic talents may achieve quite a bit when persistently following the path that God directs. Most of my work involved the rural common folks of Thailand but indirectly the life of the King was touched as told later in a later chapter.

As this preface is being composed in the year 2013 the rural and jungle areas where I worked have been dramatically changed. So it may be that there are some who may wish to get a glimpse of how life was during that period of the past. Where we once struggled with our loads of medicine over jungle trails and wading rivers there are now daily air-conditioned tour buses arriving daily at the same destinations.

DEDICATION

This book is dedicated first to "The Mother of Rural Medicine in Thailand." This lady, born a commoner, became the mother of two kings of Thailand. The present king H.M. King Bumidol Adulyadej is the longest reigning king of Thailand. Her Royal Highness Somdej Phra Sri Nakarindra Baromraj Chonni known as The Princess Mother studied nursing is Thailand then did graduate study in nursing and preventive medicine.

In the early days of our service in Thailand the land was plagued by Communist insurgents creating uncertainty as to the future of the kingdom. The Princess Mother had during those times a rigorous schedule of visiting her people, including rural areas, demonstrating concern as well as enlisting their support for the struggle against Communism. It was on one of those visits that we had a brief encounter with the Princess Mother as she visited Sangklaburi, one of the most remote areas of the kingdom. Her journey in this life included 95 action-packed years all of which were filled with service to others.

The Princess Mother with daughter to her left at school dedication in Sangklaburi.

Secondly, this book is dedicated to Olive Pa and his wife Olive Mo whom we came to know and appreciate for their dedicated service to the "least" as they served as hostel parents for the Kwai River Christian Mission. Probably no two people have done as much as they for their beloved Karen people. Olive Pa was once Minister of Education for Burma, spoke on behalf of the Karen people before British Parliament, spent time in prison; then in the later period of their lives dedicated their time and energy to the jungle children of the Karen and Thai people in the Sangklaburi area.

Olive Pa with John to his right when he was about 95 years old. Regretfully I have no photo of Olive Mo.

GRATITUDE

Nancy, my wonderful wife and companion, was the secret to my enduring the episodes, some of which were painful, during the days in Thailand. She at first distinguished herself by learning the difficult Thai language (while having a baby) easily and with a competence far beyond mine even after ten years in Thailand. She endured the deprivations of remote places with gracious patience. In Sangklaburi we were about as remote from civilization as possible in Thailand. Our home in Tapsai, while working with the Cambodian refugees, was more like a communal guest house as Nancy was at the same time teaching Krista and Jonlyn. She took Lloyd and Andrew off to India to boarding school and traveling in India without a man was a act of bravery in itself.

Nancy shared my commitment to God's calling and for that I am deeply grateful. She could write her own version of Jungle Episodes.

John and Nancy in Karen home woven clothes.

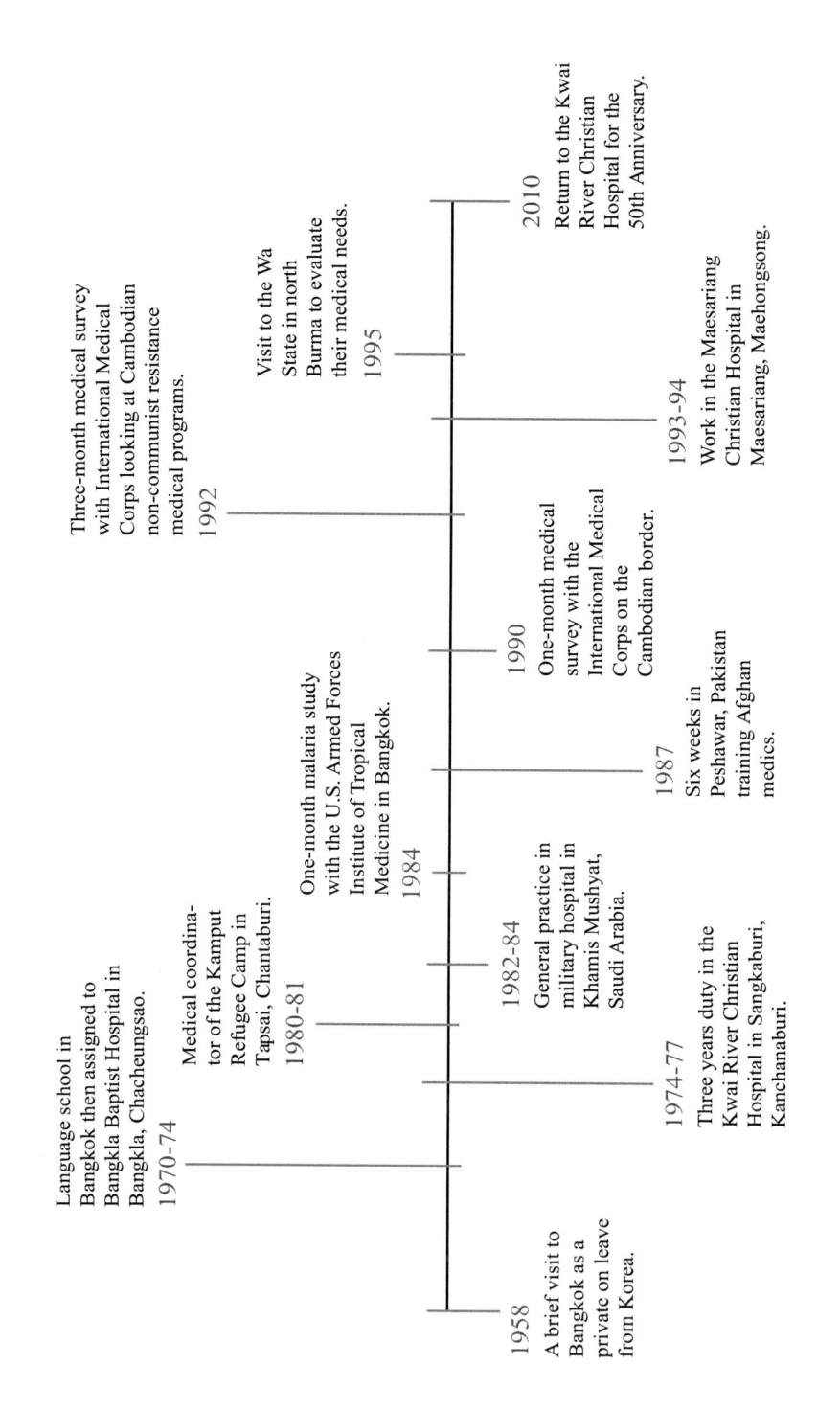

PERIODS OVERSEAS COVERED IN THIS BOOK

1958 — A brief visit to Bangkok as a private on leave from Korea.

1970-74 — Language school in Bangkok then assigned to Bangkla Baptist Hospital in Bangkla, Chacheungsao.

1974-77 — Three years duty in the Kwai River Christian Hospital in Sangkaburi, Kanchanaburi.

1980-81 — Medical coordinator of the Kamput Refugee Camp in Tapsai, Chantaburi.

1982-84 — General practice in military hospital in Khamis Mushyat, Saudi Arabia.

1984 — One-month malaria study with the U.S. Armed Forces Institute of Tropical Medicine in Bangkok.

1987 — Six weeks in Peshawar, Pakistan training Afghan medics.

1990 — One-month medical survey with the International Medical Corps on the Cambodian border.

1992 — Three-month medical survey with International Medical Corps looking at Cambodian non-communist resistance medical programs.

1993-94 — Work in the Maesariang Christian Hospital in Maesariang, Maehongsong.

1995 — Visit to the Wa State in north Burma to evaluate their medical needs.

2010 — Return to the Kwai River Christian Hospital for the 50th Anniversary.

THE PATH OF GOD'S CHOOSING

Each one of us listens to God in his own way influenced by his own cluster of associates and events. It was during my junior year in high school when the calling of God was heard and I felt that the "calling to preach." Several of the influences may be mentioned but even this group would not be the whole story. My mother prayed for me and set an excellent example in her devotion to God and willingness at ever occasion to serve others. My father though not a "church person" during my growing up regularly admonished me to "be somebody." During high school we had a very good pastor, Bro. Crabb whose memory I still cherish. My uncle John from whence comes my name regularly communicated with me and was interested that I carry on his good name. Many teachers struggled to academically inform me and one of these stands out that being Bertha Harper who was my third grade teacher and Sunday school teacher. Being in the right places one has a greater opportunity to become spiritually informed.

Choosing a college was one of the more important chores of the senior year in high school. The backdrop for this chore was the situation in which my father was absent and not working so contributed very little to the family finances. During that year it was mostly my odd jobs that kept the family finances in order. I was thus faced with college by being on my own. That didn't seem like an obstacle to be feared for somewhere along the way I had picked up enough faith to make that problem of minor importance. Wayland Baptist College in the small Panhandle town of Plainview was chosen as the site to further my ministerial education. There I was admitted on a ministerial scholarship, which meant that I was responsible for twenty-five dollars in tuition each semester as well as all other expenses.

The summer work before college paid very little but at the end of the summer Bro Crabb needed help putting a new hardwood floor in the auditorium of the church. For that job I was paid $125, which was what I had in my pocket when I boarded the train in Corpus Christi one evening as I headed for Wayland College. Tuition took $25 and room and board $60, which left me enough to buy books. They informed me that I had arrived a day late for the mandatory I.Q. test. After a bit of discussion they allowed me to proceed since I had already arrived and paid the tuition. I never had any desire to make up that test as I couldn't see that it would contribute to my self esteem so the matter of the I.Q test was laid to rest as I began inquiring about jobs.

The courses I signed up for were all in the morning leaving afternoons and Saturdays for working. After a few short time jobs working for my roommate in his Dixie Dog stand and at the local bean cannery I noticed on the job notice board a opening for a carpenter's helper. That was the bonanza that I had been praying for as James Boney had just completed his new house directly across the street from our dormitory and I could ride with him to work each afternoon following lunch. James took me in like a little brother and for three years I worked with him in his construction business, which involved small jobs. What I earned paid all my expenses and a little left over.

There were very few smooth places in my learning cycles at Wayland but I assumed that was the way it was supposed to be. The failure of my speech course was of course a blow to my ego. A couple of roommates, one from China and one from Costa Rica, broadened my horizons to the international scene. Then a mission conference featuring an "old China hand" by the name of Jim Graham was held on the campus. The result of that was my decision to go into missions. Dr. Lee's biology class proved to be another career-changing experience. In our small classes Dr. Lee knew most of us and our plans so when he observed that I excelled in biology he asked one day if I had ever considered becoming a medical missionary. That got me to thinking and as I remembered my poor showing in speech class and some of the Bible classes the drift toward a premed program looked more inviting.

After three years at Wayland and with my mind made up to study medicine I decided to transfer to the University of Texas where there would be broader range of pre-med courses. That was probably a mistake as what should have been my senior year dragged on until my graduation in 1961 making my college time a full ten years. Uncle Sam called me during that time for a tour in Korea. Following that episode there was some doubt about my future so when released by Uncle Sam I taught school a year. During that period of uncertainty I decided to attend Southwestern Baptist Seminary in Ft. Worth, Texas.

Everything was ready for that move including a part time job at the seminary when God informed me through a strong feeling that such was not the right direction. At the end of my one-year career of teaching the sixth grade I found myself headed to Denver to work with my brother in the construction business, still not knowing just what lay in the future.

After about two months in Denver I attended a Layman's Crusade in one of the Baptist churches. On the way home from that meeting there was an intense feeling that I should continue preparation for medical school. During my last semester in the University of Texas I had taken the Medical College Admission Test (MCAT) and did so poorly that it cast a serious cloud on my medical career aspirations. The feeling that I should resume studies to prepare for medical school were so strong and persistent that I enrolled in the University of Denver to complete a few pre-med requirements.

Near the end of that academic year I retook the MCAT and applied to several medical schools. The replies from the schools were again disheartning with one school telling me not to bother sending in an application as I would be wasting my money. My MCAT score was not impressive and neither were my grades. The result of my last semester at the University of Texas was every grade in the book. Every course that had math in it had to be repeated making me a very poor candidate for a medical school. Naturally the doubts about a medical career returned and I started searching again for God's path.

The Baptist Student Union of the University of Denver initiated their first Summer Missionary Program that summer and their candidate at the last minute canceled. They asked me if I could fill in and since my hopes for medical school were dashed I assented. During the summer in California I was pondering my future and had several graduate application forms in my bag. When I tried to fill them out there was something that told me not to. Having concluded my duties with the mission work there began a series of prompting that I can only ascribe to God. First was the impression that I should return to Denver promptly so the ticket was confirmed and the end of summer mission formalities were skipped. On the plane to Denver again was a sudden feeling that I should go talk to the Dean of the University of Colorado Medical School about the possibility of applying when I had established residency. At the Denver airport I called the Dean's office and was invited to come that day; which I did.

The Dean listened very graciously to my story then asked me if I would like to go to medical school that Fall. Before I could answer his phone rang and I had time to sit and think while he talked. I pondered, he talked, and I knew that God was working. When his telephone conversation was over he handed me the name of the dean of the University of South Dakota and the telephone number. He had just the day before talked to Dean Hard and had been informed the there were seven sudden vacancies in the program of South Dakota. I thanked him and left to pursue that path. Soon all the information needed had been mailed to the University of South Dakota and I anxiously waited.

The next week on Friday afternoon I was doing some carpenter repair work in the University Baptist Church when the pastor announced a phone call for me. It was South Dakota calling to ask if I wanted to be in their Fall class which was to begin on Monday.

My financial situation was, well there was no financial situation as I had worked all summer for nothing there was no one I could turn to for help. My car was sold to get a few hundred dollars enough to pay the first semester $500 tuition. Henry, my brother's partner gave me a used worn out microscope. I called to get a ticket to Vermillion, South Dakota, only to discover that there was no way to get there from Denver on public transportation. My brother Alva seeing my predicament finally volunteered to drive me to my destination.

The sudden last minute openings in South Dakota appeared due to many students applying to several schools then when admitted to their first choice they cancel their second choice, the two-year medical school of South Dakota. South Dakota at that time only had a school with the basic sciences making it necessary to transfer to another school for the last two years. And so it was that God had that way of accomplishing his purpose for me. God had endowed me with a bit of faith and also a dose of persistence as I kept responding to His nudgings.

Getting admitted to medical school was only the beginning of the struggle. My four sisters had proclaimed, that, "John has no business going to medical school for he neither has good sense nor money." And they were right but God provides and in spite of working my way through school I managed to avoid the flunk-outs at the bottom of the class which were quite a few. As one of my classmates said, "We got under the wire but with plenty of scratches on our backs."

We can lean back and rest on God's leading for it is surely in our favor. The University of South Dakota Medical School at that time was the most inexpensive in the country and that was what I needed. The classes were small so there was good interchange between student and faculty. The students all knew one another and were helpful to each other. It was the perfect place for a person with "not good sense and no money."

From South Dakota I transferred to the University of Tennessee in Memphis for the remaining two years. When I arrived to enroll I was informed that since my mother was residing in Tennessee I would be charged resident tuition. That was in spite of the fact that I had not lived in Tennessee before. Again God provided for the financial part of my education. In Memphis I met Nancy Davis, which led to romance. We were married at the time of my graduation. Following that was internship in Methodist Hospital Memphis then a year of practice in South Dakota then a year of surgery training in Baylor Hospital in Dallas. During the year at Baylor Hospital Nancy and I were commissioned as missionaries to Thailand

LANGUAGE SCHOOL INTERMISSION

The Bangkok language studies had been in progress for about a year. There was no problem for me to understand the need to acquire a working knowledge of the second most difficult language in the world with its multiple tones that could if mispronounced completely reverse the meaning one had intended. Nevertheless it was extremely hard on my psychology to be in a classroom eight hours a day for five days a week. The weekend working visits to the Bangkla Baptist Hospital two hours drive to the east where I would eventually be posted broke up the tedious language study a bit and gave me opportunity to practice in a real setting what I was learning. Those twice a month trips didn't completely assuage my feelings of "institutional fever" which had infected me on previous occasions. Further galling the situation was Nancy's natural linguistic ability demonstrated by her perfect tones and within a short time the ability to read the most complex Thai novel.

The situation in East Pakistan at that time caught my attention for a college friend from Wayland had already been for several years a missionary in that Muslim country. The typhoon in 1970 was the most devastating in the history of that area resulting in the deaths of about one half million poor villagers. Jim McKinley's town of Comilla had been included in the path of destruction. We read accounts of his heroic and continuous efforts to help the people with relief work one part being drilling wells in many villages so fresh water could be provided. The country had not recovered from the typhoon when the Bengali people began moves to relieve themselves of the West Pakistani oppression.

The Muslim country of Pakistan comprising the West and East parts resulted from the Indian partition of 1948. The dominant force was the West Pakistanis who were influenced by the fierce tall tribal Pashtoon mountain people. They were quite a contrast to the smaller peaceful Bengali people who were a mixture of Buddhist, Hindu, and some Christians. The dominant Muslim West persistently dominated and oppressed their Eastern countrymen to the point where independence was declared in March of 1970 and a war of rebel resistance began.

December approached with the situation in East Pakistan heating up and my confinement in language school resulting in more restlessness. Compassion for my friend Jim and Betty McKinley and his small children prompted me to the decision to make a Santa Claus run to Dacca with a load of Christmas candy and toys for his children for I knew those things would be difficult to obtain in that country. With my roundtrip ticket on Pakistani Airways I was off to Dacca where Jim and his family were then living.

When customs was completed I gave Jim's address to a taxi driver and we were off to find his Baptist compound. We passed several anti-aircraft batteries with their guns pointed to the sky. The streets were mostly deserted due to the palpable tension in the atmosphere. India had decided to get involved in support of the breakaway Mukti Bahini (freedom fighters) forces. At the same time the West Pakistanis had seriously reinforced their positions in the country. It was easy to distinguish the tall fierce looking West Pakistanis from the shorter and slightly oriental looking Bengalis. Jim met me at the locked compound gate and greeted me with mixed feelings. He then filled me in on the situation, which could develop in several rather dire directions.

Before bedtime we walked next door to visit the Thurmans who had also been in East Pakistan for several years. It had to be at least eight years for Mrs. Thurman had contracted leprosy and had been treated for that malady. She was the only missionary I have known who had been afflicted with that once dreaded disease. Their problem at that time was involved with protecting their near puberty girls from the predatory nature of the neighbor Muslim young boys. Apparently time is not wasted on the teaching of the necessity of sexual discipline on males in the Muslim culture. We returned to Jim's house and went to bed for a good night's sleep.

Sleep was good until about one AM when a distant loud explosion that sent a tremor through our house was heard. We were all up immediately discussing the source of what was certainly an bomb for a lone airplane was heard in the distance. Then later in the morning it was announced that the airport was closed. I had been on the last civilian flight into Dacca. About noon another event caught our attention as Indian and Pakistani jet fighters were engaged in a dogfight directly over the city. Flashes of light could be seen coming from one jet then a few seconds later another jet would go into a spiral and next would be an opening parachute. That went on for a couple of days until the weaker Pakistan air force was spent.

With the Indians in full control of the air the next sounds were of the Indian planes attacking Pakistani positions in different parts of Dacca. We could see the Indian jets as they came in low aiming for their targets. Then there would be a rip-roaring sound as the rockets tore into Pakistani positions. Of course there was a bit of apprehension as we considered that one of them could get off course and we would be the victims of one of the raids. Those attacks went on for several days, as Dacca was the final destination of the Indian army in collusion with the Mukti Bahini (freedom fighters).

During those days there was a continual stream of people rattling Jim's locked gate. Jim would go out and talk for a few minutes with them and then come back and report on what was going on. One visitor had a distinctly oriental look that aroused my curiosity. He was a Naga from the hills of Eastern India. His tribe had been evangelized many years earlier, by American Baptist missionaries, and now were a strongly Christian ethnic group. Interestingly before becoming Christians during the British era they were headhunters. They viewed the Indians as oppressive and had for some years been trying to become an independent state. The man that day was one of group who had been receiving military training by the Pakistanis so naturally he was apprehensive as to their situation should the Indians succeed in the war. Others came just to get news as they knew that the little Baptist compound had radios.

Jim told me of the Razakar Biharis who were shedding their uniforms while trying to blend into the native population. The Biharis were Muslims who had lived in India before partition and were forced to move into East Pakistan The Pakistanis thought they would be a safe group to enlist in a paramilitary force so they had been on the side of the oppressive Pakistanis. Now they were in jeopardy as were other groups who had been too cooperative with the Pakistanis.

With the cessation of "air traffic" over the city calmness prevailed causing me to begin to think of a way to get back to Bangkok. Howard Teal, another Baptist missionary to Pakistan but caught visiting as I had been was also looking for a way out. We decided one morning to go to the International Hotel, which was the place most likely to get information about travel. Pakistan had conceded defeat so there was celebration in the air as commandeered pickup truck loads of Mukti Bahini roared through the streets firing their guns into the air and shouting,

"Joy Bangla."

Howard and I were standing in front of the hotel watching and talking when on the right a armored column of the Indian Army came to a halt at the intersection. At about the same time coming down the street from the right and marching in front of the Indians was a column of surrendering Pakistani troops still fully armed. The Mukti Bahini continued to race around punctuating that very tense situation. The explosive nature of that situation finally seized me and I grabbed Howard's arm and said, "Let's get around behind this building to a safer place." No sooner had we gotten into the inner part of the Hotel when all hell broke loose. Someone in that tense situation got spooked and shots were fired killing the commander of the Indian forces who was desperately trying to stop the firing. Several Pakistanis were also killed before calm was restored.

When calm prevailed a USAID worker was dragged in from in front of the building who had been caught in the crossfire. From somewhere a first aid kit with surgical instruments appeared and I was in business sewing up the lacerations across his back that had been caused by a passing bullet. He had been in about the same place where Howard and I were standing a few moments before.

We learned that an Indian army helicopter would be leaving the next morning and if we were at the airport we might get on it. On the drive to the airport we passed bodies here and there on the streets more than likely from revenge killings. The anti-aircraft guns were now lowered to horizontal positions and at time aimed directly at us, resulting in an erie feeling. The Pakistani crews were not leaving the security of their positions until picked up by the proper Indian authorities.

Howard and I did get a seat on the Russian made troop-carrying helicopter. Among the other passengers was Peter Jennings and his camera crew as at that time he was posted in Hong Kong but covering the war. We were deposited in the Indian city of Argatala which was on the eastern border of the new country of Bangladesh. The night in the mosquito infested city of Argatala without a mosquito net left me with what looked like chicken pox. The next day we caught an Indian Airlines flight to Calcutta. There I went about trying to get to Bangkok without proper documentation and with a worthless Pakistan Airlines ticket and no money. Peter Jennings' cameraman was gracious enough to lend me ticket money so that problem was solved.

The dining room in the Calcutta hotel where we stayed was that night hosting the Indian Air Force pilots whom we had seen in the dogfights over Dacca. It was interesting to watch them as they lifted their glasses in celebration of their victory. I joined Peter Jennings and his crew to enjoy the show.

The few dollars I had left managed to grease my way though Indian immigration and onto the plane which took Howard and I to Bangkok where I arrived in time for Christmas. That little escapade cured my restlessness for the remainder of the year and half of language school.

A BRIDGE OVER THE UPPER KWAI

Note: This episode was documented in 1977 soon after completion of the bridge as a report to the American Women's Club of Bangkok and the American Baptist Mission both of whom contributed funds to make the bridge possible. It has been revised with additions since then.

TRAVEL ON THE KWAI

At 5:45 in the morning it was barely peeping daylight in the Kanchanaburi railroad station where we stood watching the wood burning antique steam engine smoking and blowing off excess steam. The children were eating kao lam (roasted sticky rice in bamboo) while Nancy and I ate from a small sack of fresh pineapple. Other vendors had a good selection of foods from which we completed our breakfast. There was not a large crowd so when the conductor motioned to board there was not a great rush. Only a few government workers and timber merchants had business on the Kwai River in those days.

On the way to the railroad station that morning we had passed in the near darkness the outline of the Kanchanaburi War Cemetery where thousands of identical military tombstones lay row upon row. On those stones were inscribed the names of thousands of British and Dutch war prisoners who had perished in building the infamous "Death Railway" in the early forties. The Japanese had pushed their military frontier into Burma but by that time the sea lanes were controlled by Allied submarines so there was an urgent push to connect the rail lines in Kanchanaburi to Moulmein in Burma so their military campaign could be supplied overland. British engineers in preWWII times had looked at the possibility of a railroad to connect Thailand and Burma but the formidable mountain terrain had nixed their plans.

Japanese engineers looked at the situation from a different standpoint and concluded that it could be done. Massive numbers of laborers were needed so British and Dutch POWs along with indigenous workers from Malaysia, Burma and India were conscripted for the project. The 250 kilometer line was completed in record time but at

A steam engine similar to this pulled our train into the jungle. Left to right: Lloyd, Andrew, Krista, and Jonlyn (1980).

the cost of one death per railroad sleeper that was put in place; that amounted to over 100,000 disposable souls.

Promptly at six o'clock the steam whistle blew and the chugging of the narrow gauge locomotive commenced. We were on our way to reopen the Kwai River Christian Hospital which lay at the headwaters of the Kwai River on the Thai-Burma border very near the site where the railroad had briefly crossed into Burma. The little ten-bed hospital/clinic had been constructed in the early sixties to serve the people living in that remote and isolated area. The American Baptists had many years of experience working with the hilltribes in Burma and India, so when they came to Thailand they naturally migrated to the Thai hilltribes to do missionary work. The Kwai River hospital had been closed for about three years due to the lack of a missionary doctor. We were moving there with the intention to concentrate on community health as a way to improve the health of the villagers in that area.

Just as the sun was showing over the Eastern horizon, we approached the Bridge over the Kwai. This was the bridge built by the Japanese in WWII using Allied prisoners and made famous by the movie <u>The Bridge Over the River Kwai</u>. Contrary to the movie version, the bridge was not destroyed by commandos, nor were there any documented escapes by Allied prisoners from the camps. The bridge we crossed that morning was constructed from materials taken from Indonesia and transported to this more essential location. There were two odd spans in the bridge, which were replacements for the ones destroyed by American B-24 bombers flying from India. The Allies kept watch by aerial reconnaissance as the railroad was being constructed then as it neared completion began their bombing.

This was the dry season so the trip up the Eastern edge of the Little Kwai River to the end of the rail line would take the customary two hours as the wood would be dry for the locomotive. This section from Kanchanaburi to Saiyoke was all that remained of the "Death Railroad". The rest of the line had been so poorly constructed and so damaged by the Allied bombing that it was not considered feasible to repair it at the end of the war. Our little train crept along at the speed of about thirty miles per hour over rickety trestles and poorly maintained rails. At one place we could look straight down at the slow-moving

Unlike the movie version this is the Bridge over the River Kwai.

water of the Kwai, clear blue at this time in the dry season. The trestles could be seen moving and swaying, an eerie feeling. Sugarcane plantations dotted the landscape, which soon gave way to more frontier-looking small farms. We made a few stops at isolated stations then pulled into Saiyoke station.

All our baggage was removed from the train and porters engaged to move the stuff the short distance to the river where we negotiated for a long-tailed boat, to take us to Takanun. The boats are called long-tailed because the propeller shaft is twenty feet long, extending directly from a used truck diesel engine that sits atop the stern of the boat. It is steered by the driver who cradles the front of the engine in his lap. Steering is by swiveling the engine on its mount. Conversation on the boats is very limited due to the noise of the mufflerless motor. The boats are wide enough for two adults to sit side by side, there being about ten to twelve rows of seats. After about an hour, we were situated in our boat and ready for the four or five-hour boat ride up river.

Fried rice had been purchased at the floating café, so our first chore was to enjoy a late breakfast that had been wrapped in banana leaves. The scenery on the Kwai was as beautiful as the noise was noxious. The cloudless blue skies matched the clear blue of the river. At bends of the river were large white sand bars, which the children looked on with envy. Limestone clefts decorated with tropical vegetation, some seeming to be one hundred feet high, lined the banks. A waterfall dropped into the river now and then. Except for the noise, we enjoyed that trip along the most beautiful river that I have ever traveled. The boats of course had no "facilities" so when a person needed relief he would raise his hand and point to the bank, or he may yell "Pout tong eiew (My belly hurts I want to pee)." The boat driver would then look for an appropriate place to stop.

In that spring of 1974, there was little on the Kwai other than nature's beauty. Every now and then, there would be a small house floating on a bamboo raft. Two or three times we saw an elephant or two pulling teak logs down to the river. Water monkeys swing from the trees along the river bank and once one was seen swimming across the river. We sat on seats only four inches above the floor boards, so after five hours, Nancy and I had had enough of the beauty of the Kwai and were much relieved when the little riverside market town of Takanun

One of the many waterfalls on the Kwai River.

A white sand beach in a bend of the Kwai.

An elephant logging on the bank of the Kwai River.

came into sight. Lloyd and Andy with Krista tagging along set out to explore the shore while we unloaded the boat. Jonlyn was only six months old so she was in our arms. The name of a shop with rooms to rent had been given to us, so we went looking for that shop as we would need to spend the night before proceeding to Sangklaburi by truck.

Fortunately the rooms were available, for we had a large group which included my sister Cathy and her two small children, Michelle and Curry, who were on an extended visit at that time. Our Thai housekeeper, Eiam, was also moving with us. The upstairs rooms were clean, spacious and overlooking the river. As soon as the family was settled, I set out to look for a truck that would carry us through the jungle the next day. We were well into the dry season so the river was too low to allow boats to navigate the remaining distance to Sangklaburi. That evening we had supper made from wild pig meat, quite tasty and tender.

There was no road to Sangklaburi, so no scheduled means of transportation. Eventually I made a deal with the owner of an ex-army four-wheel drive pickup (well it had originally been a four-wheel drive). Thinking that we would leave about seven in the morning, we had everything loaded and ready to go. After a long delay, it was finally discovered that the driver was waiting, hoping to get some more paying passengers. It was mid morning when we finally left Takanun and within a few minutes we were in the jungle. The driver was experienced, so he knew the right paths to take as well as the best places to cross the creeks. For some reason the truck died in the middle of a muddy creek bed, which generated a bit of activity. It turned out that the truck didn't have a clutch, so the rear wheel was jacked up so that when the engine started, it could be shifted into low gear. Every truck I ever rode on through that jungle had some "essential" part missing.

The midway point was Wangpatoe, a sleepy and miserable looking village with a shop or two. I later found that the inhabitants were about as miserable as the village looked. We had lunch there of a poor grade of the famous Thai noodle soup, which with its congealed blood and chicken head didn't make it an enjoyable experience. By this time we were well out of range of electricity and ice so the hot Fanta drinks added very little to alleviate our fatigue. Leaving Wangpatoe we immediately encountered the really rough going. We had to hold on with both hands receiving repeated spine jarring jolts when the wheels slipped into deep ruts. A later visitor who came to the hospital as a leprosy specialist claimed that he suffered a fractured vertebra on that "road". I had devised a hammock for Jonlyn made of a pakama (long cloth men use as wraparound trousers). Jonlyn never seemed to mind as she rolled back and forth like a wheel in her sling.

SANGKLABURI

After five hours of breathing and eating dust while being bounced about mercilessly, I caught a glimpse of houses made of wood with a bit of artistic embellish in their construction. We had entered the Mon village, one part of Sangklaburi. We had a brief stop in this place peopled with Mon refugees from the brutal regime in Burma. After stretching our legs, we loaded again and went down to cross the river, about running board depth at this time of the year. On the Karen side of the river, we passed some more scattered houses and shops, not nearly as neat as the Mon, before crossing the Rantee a tributary of the Kwai. The hospital was located on the bank of the Rantee so within a few minutes we pulled up at the "Doctor's House."

Sangklaburi, the county seat, is located where three small rivers converge to form the Little Kwai. The Rantee flows from an easterly direction with our mission compound located on its northern bank. To the west of us the Songkalia branch came from the north and joined the Rantee just below the hospital. A few hundred yards further down and just above the Mon village the Beke joined coming in from the west. These were all clear water rivers and navigable up to the hospital except in the three driest months. Just a few minutes walk from the hospital was the remains of a rail yard that was the midpoint of the "Death Railroad." It had a repair yard, turnaround, and service facilities for the trains that carried supplies into Burma for the Japanese army. Other than the foundation stones all that remained when we arrived was a steam road packer and an iron flatbed railcar.

It wasn't long before Nancy and Eiam had the house organized for living, so that left me to look into getting the hospital reopened. Josie Fallow, an Australian Baptist missionary nurse, had already been working in the hospital for several months, so she had it cleaned and had put together a staff of local folks who had worked there before. I agreed with Josie that the focus of the medical work there should be on public health and preventive medicine. The villages were scattered and people operated on a barter economy leaving very little money for expensive hospital care. Most of the diseases were due to malaria and intestinal parasites, which would be amenable to a public health program. A village health program was started with Olivia, a trained midwife/public health worker in charge. It was so effective in preventing diseases that soon I had no reason to go on the trips to villages.

At first we had only a few patients in the hospital as patients did not come to the hospital except in extremis, and when they were that sick, they were too sick to travel. Transportation was often more costly than could be afforded. Ebra was a nurse trained in one of the old mission hospitals in Burma. She knew every detail of hospital work and was an excellent clinician as well, so with her and Josie, things went well in our little ten bed hospital, where we cared for patients suffering from bear and elephant attacks, snake bites, cerebral malaria and hookworm anemia.

TALK OF A BRIDGE

A year or so had gone by when I heard a rumor that the government planned to build a bridge over the Rantee that would connect our compound with the rest of the town of Sangklaburi. In the dry season, people could wade across the river, but in the rainy season, it required boats which added to the expense of getting to the hospital, and of course more dangerous for the students attending our mission school. One night a birth complicated by retained placenta occurred on the other side of the river. Births in that area were usually celebrated by a generous amount of moonshine rice whiskey. In the process of getting to the hospital, the baby was dropped in the river. Fortunately the child was retrieved with no harm. The mother recovered as well. A bridge would lessen our sense of isolation which was enough already in that back side of nowhere.

Hearing that the Nai Amphur (District executive officer) was present for his monthly visit, I ventured over to the government offices to lend the mission's support to the idea of a bridge as well as to gain particulars of the project. He allowed that the rumor was indeed true and the contract would be let soon. When asked about the type of bridge the Nai Amphur told me that it would be made of jungle timber with a center span made of steel using the old "Death Railroad" rails that had been squirreled away in the jungle at the end of the WWII by some enterprising locals. "Who is going to build the center span?" I asked. The Nai Amphur had no idea. Knowing that no one in that part of the jungle had any knowledge of building a steel span of that nature, I on a spur of the moment inspiration, volunteered to take responsibility for that part of the bridge. He agreed if that suited the local who received the contract for the bridge.

A few days later, I happened upon Kamnan (district headman) Tun who had received the contract to build the bridge. He was probably the only one in the area with the skills needed for the project, as he was an old timber merchant. Being of a pleasant nature to deal with he was, as well, wily as a fox. Kamnan Tun was a young man during the days of the Japanese occupation and watched as they built the railroad through that area. I told him of my conversation with the Nai Amphur and the offer to build the center span. Whether he thought I could do that or not, he didn't let on but went on to offer to get all the rails that would be needed. He knew everything about the jungle where the rails had been cached away and who they belonged to.

Nancy was not at all impressed with my offer to help with the bridge. Being the mother of four small children in the jungle wasn't an easy job at all. There was home schooling every day, which took a bit of preparation. The children had never been to school before, so didn't know how to act, consequently they were reluctant learners. Perhaps they were overly tempted by the small river in front of our house, where they practically lived. But that was a concern as well since at that time Krista and Jonlyn were young enough to accidentally fall in and be swept away especially in flood season.

The food supply was a chronic problem as well. There was no market so we had to grow our own food. It seemed that every night something would bother Nancy's chickens so she had to wake up and see about them. We lived on the end of the line for the fresh meat vendors, so were left out most of the time leaving us feasting frequently on canned sardines and rice. Not being cut out for house work or teaching, I pressed on with the bridge project.

Immediately I began trying to figure out how to get the bridge built. My years of carpentering helped a little, but never had I worked with steel. Kamnam Tun showed me one of the rails that we would use. I measured it and traced off a cross-section then wrote to my mining engineer brother in Denver telling him that we needed simple blueprints for an eighty foot long (two rail lengths) bridge that would hold up a fully loaded ten wheel truck. About a month later blueprints came from the Mile High Engineering Co., friends of my brother Alva. It looked like a workable design, but there were many details that were left out such as how to connect the rails together-welding or bolting?

Technical advice was hard to come by in the jungle as we had no telephone, telegraph nor radio at that time. One didn't just jump up and run to Bangkok any old time as going and coming would use up the better part of a week and was very expensive. As soon as possible I conjured up a trip to Bangkok to buy supplies for the hospital. For the bridge there were needs as well, such as money, technical advice and tools. It was nearing the beginning of the rainy season. It would take all of the rainy season to get the steel prepared, then we could use the dry season when there would be hardly any water in the river for the construction process.

While in Bangkok I discussed the project with Cecil Carder, the mission administrator who produced approval to use the money that had been set aside for an erosion prevention project for our mission station. I had planted local water bushes along our bank of the river, which was doing a good job of erosion control. The American Women's Club of Bangkok gave a couple of thousand dollars. At the International Church that Sunday, I met an engineer teaching at the Asia Institute of Technology in Bangkok. He was immediately pulled away and questions were thrown at him mainly about the manner of putting the steel together. After our discussion it was decided that the most practical thing to do in the jungle was to drill and bolt the steel together. He would not venture to advise me on the number of bolts for each joint, but offered to test the bolts on his school's shear test machine. From that we determined how many tons of weight each one half inch bold would support.

The Bangkok Christian Hospital's administrator and maintenance director had already helped in solving many problems for our hospital, so I went to them to seek assistance with the tools. Sure enough I

Bridge construction shack in front of hospital.

went to the right place for I came away with an old power hack saw in perfect working condition and hoping that it would cut the rails as intended. Included was a heavy duty drill press that would come in handy. The mission offered the use of an antique Lister one cylinder diesel generator that was not in use at the time. I found out later why it was not in use. A heavy duty one half inch drill purchased in the market completed the tool inventory. We endured our return to Sangklaburi confident that the bridge project was underway.

BRIDGE CONSTRUCTION

As soon as we had recuperated from the Bangkok trip, I went to work on the bridge. With no engineering skills, I drew to scale the essential joints of the bridge on our Christian school's cement floor. From those drawings I then used half inch plywood to make full scale models of the various joint plates that would be used to connect the rails. On the next trip to Bangkok, those models were taken to the best welder I could find who perfectly duplicated the wooded models using half inch steel.

The next chore was to get the rails delivered and start cutting them to the proper length. For this process a shelter was erected in front of the hospital, where the drill press was set up on a track where the rails could be moved as they were drilled. The nurses didn't like the looks of that uncouth shack, but I could supervise the work easily from the hospital. Our little Lister generator was a disappointment as it belched black smoke and refused to produce a volt of electricity. The local mechanic was enlisted to take a look at it. He took it apart and said it needed a new set of rings. The parts were obtained but Puong never returned. He had been last sighted in Three Pagoda Pass working on a rice mill. Puong had been treated earlier in our hospital for cerebral malaria and it had been said that his brain was softened by the illness.

Gloom hung over the bridge shack as the generator lay dissected, no rails had materialized and I had no person who knew how to do steel work. Then two sightseeing visitors arrived at the hospital one Wednesday afternoon. Paul and Tom were Americans living in Bangkok, between jobs, who were taking the opportunity of sightseeing the Kwai and Three Pagoda Pass, then a tourist site for more adventurous souls. When I found that Paul was a diesel mechanic and Tom was a musician with skills in piano tuning, those two tourists were immediately invited to stay for a few days. After hearing of my dilemma, Paul immediately set to work the next morning repairing the generator. Emilie, our senior missionary, had collected piano strings and tuning tools for the repair of the Christian Hostel piano that Olive Moe, the hostel mother, continued to use in a wonderful way in her work with the children from the villages.

Saturday night Olive Moe with the help of Olive Pa had organized a musical concert accompanied by a piano which was perfectly tuned for the first time in years. Tom even played some beautiful pieces as part of the program. Of course there was a special meal that was enjoyed by all of the mission folks. Even our piano had been tuned for the first time since it had arrived in Thailand. Paul had the generator running smoothly and producing the proper number of watts and volts. When in the jungle, one learns to live by faith and it is pleasant to look back and see how God provided when things looked hopeless. We never heard from Paul or Tom again, perhaps they were angels.

A truckload of rails appeared a few days later that caused more dismay than delight. They were all bent, some of them in several directions. Apparently those rails were from railroad trestles that had either been bombed by Allied planes or burned at some time during the annual slash and burn fires that the mountain villagers used to clear their rice fields. They had lain there for about a week when Nai (Mr.) Chert came to visit me at the hospital. He had heard that we were going to build a bridge so he came inquiring about working some on it in order to pay off a hospital bill he had incurred as a result of an abscessed tooth. We stood there in front of the hospital talking a bit when he inquired about the pile of twisted rails. "Those will be sold for scrap," I informed him, as they were worthless for anything else.

Nai Chert was a short bandy-legged man with a mustache, which began to twitch as he surveyed the rails. His eyes sparkled as he told me matter-of-factly that he might be able to straighten out some of them. That immediately got my attention, for I had forgotten that he was known for his blacksmithing skills, as well as being a farmer. I thought a minute and then remembered the man who had paid his hospital bill the previous week with ten beeps (a beep is a five gallon tin) of charcoal which could be used to fire the forge. Nai Chert went back to Beke, about a half days walk away, to get his billows and other tools.

Years later Nai Chert related to me how he happened to have moved from his home in north Thailand to the Beke area. His younger brother Boonchom had been enlisted as a teacher in our little Christian school where teachers were reluctant to live due to the remote location. Boonchom taught one year then returned to his home up north for a visit. It was clear to Boonchom that the villagers in the Sangklaburi area needed teachers with a Christian witness in an area plagued with spirit worship, but Boonchom was a Sgaw Karen and the people in our area were Pwo Karen, who speak a different dialect. Sangklaburi was a challenging place, and as a single man he had found it very difficult to live there. If Nai Chert and his family would go with him, then Boonchom would go back to be a missionary to the Pwo Karen and work to get a church started there.

Nai Chert prayed then accepted his brother's challenge. His land was all sold and his family moved after they found a site in the Beke village, where he continued to support his brother Boonchom. Years later after Nai Chert's old family farm up north had skyrocketed in price, Nancy asked him if he had ever been sorry that he sold out and moved. "Never have I been sorry!" he said emphatically. Boonchom was still teaching, and he was also pastor of a thriving church.

Clinic was about over when Nai Chert came in and requested that I come out and have a look when I had time. He had put his forge at the end of the rail drilling track, making it possible for the rails to be easily rolled through the forge fire. His first rail was straight as an arrow. He and one helper had done a perfect job in short order. Nai Chert again had my attention. I asked him what he thought about the other rails. He replied that he would work on some of the less crooked ones. Within a few days, they were all straight enough to be used in the bridge construction. The only smithing work Nai Chert had ever done was making knives and plowpoints. He was hired to assist Nai Hlaing the foreman of the bridge project. Nai Hlaing had done a bit of carpenter work for the mission, and I had been impressed with his skills and precision, but he had never done any steel work. The two worked perfectly together. Nai Hlaing was a Mon who were noted for

Nai Chert's bambo church in his village of Beke.

Kamnan Tum (with tattoes), his son (shirtless), and the generator mechanic who disappeared.

their craftsmanship.

The rainy season was upon us and things were ready as I now had a good crew. The tools were all in place and working. The bent rails had been straightened, but that bunch was not nearly enough. I kept asking Kamnan Tun about the rails and he kept promising that they would be there any day. Finally loads of straight rails arrived, but again they were disappointing as there were about a dozen different kinds and sizes of rails. The Japanese did not use any new material in the construction of the railroad, but ripped up nonessential rail material from conquered countries, which was shipped in for the jungle railroad. Fortunately we were able to get enough of the forty-foot rails to use for the periphery of the two main trusses, which required two rails bolted back to back. The odd rails were used for cross bracing and places where strength was not so crucial.

One more trip had to be made to Bangkok to pick up the joint plates. Other supplies were needed as well. It would take plenty of blades for the power hacksaw as well as a large quantity of drill bits. Another last minute item was custom made beveled washers, two for each bolt, which would adjust for the bevel on the rail flanges. Kamnan Tun requested a two inch diameter steel shaft twenty feet long, which would be used in his construction of the pile driver. That was a fast trip since I didn't want to be away from the family too long.

The little shack in front of the hospital became a beehive of activity with all the cutting and drilling. We concentrated first on the two main trusses, 80 feet long and 20 feet high, that were the main components of the bridge. All of the joint plates were bolted between the two rails that made up the periphery of the trusses. Other rails would be bolted top and bottom to hold the trusses together. As no engineer would venture to advise me about the number of bolts needed in each joint, I used my own calculations based on my high school geometry and common sense. The shear test of the bolts from the Technical School helped of course. After cutting and drilling the rails they were moved down to the bridge site where the trusses were assembled lying down on a flat field. In that way we knew that when the dry season came every piece would fit, making the final assembly much easier.

Nai Chert and Nai Hlaing worked together in such efficiency that I usually made only one brief visit with them each day to discuss the bridge work. Work was moving along well and the peak of the rains was over when on one of my daily visits Nai Chert informed me that he would need a few days off to go back to his village. Elephants had gotten loose, or perhaps they were wild elephants, I don't remember, and were getting into the hillside rice fields around his area. Rice at this time was fully grown and beginning to head so it was particularly appetizing to elephants, who could clean out a field of rice in a couple of hours, which would leave a farmer destitute. The next day Nai Hlaing said that since the work was going so well, he might take a week off to visit his family in Burma. I never understood why he didn't move his family to Sangklaburi since he always had plenty of work there.

During the lull I spoke to the Kamnan about the bridge. His job was to construct the approaches to the bridge, which had a total length of one hundred meters so a goodly number of logs would be needed for pilings as well as sawn lumber for the floor of the bridge. His ancient WWII logging trucks, converted from British lorries, had been busy and were stockpiling the pilings. The trucks had been made over so many times they hardly resembled the originals, but it was amazing how they could pull loads of logs through the jungle up to their axles in that monsoon muck. The only improved road in our area was a half mile of service road that paralleled the "Death Railroad" which the prisoners had paved with rocks from the surrounding area. That made up the "main street" of Three Pagoda Pass. The Kamnan's men were already busy with axes sharpening the ends of the pilings so they could be pounded into the river bottom.

The Kamnan had another crew out in the jungle sawing mai dang (very hard and durable red wood grown in that area) into two inch thick boards. Saw mills were forbidden in our area so all lumber was sawn by hand illegally even for our bridge. The log was placed on a frame with one man on top and another in the pit underneath. A crosscut-like saw was pulled up and down by the men all day long in tedious monotony. Government timber inspectors looked the other way for a little tea money.

After about a week or ten days, Nai Chert was back having saved his rice fields from the elephants. Nai Hlaing returned from his visit about the same time so work resumed. By the end of the rains, they had completed the assembly of the two trusses and the cutting of the remainder of the steels rails. But Kamnan Tun had not started the construction of the approaches. Knowing that we would be hard pressed to complete the bridge during a single dry season, I asked him what was delaying his work. He replied that his men had not located the proper tree for the pile driver. He explained that he needed an especially tough kind of wood from which he would make the driver for his makeshift pile driver.

About two weeks later, I ventured down to the river and to my surprise, Kamnan's pile driver was at work. Kamnan Tun in his younger days had observed the Japanese building the railroad and that information had been filed away for later use when needed in that mountainous area. His pile driver was modeled on the ones remembered from that time and it seemed to be working although rather slowly. It was composed of a rickety scaffolding which held the piling in an upright position with the twenty foot steel shaft in a hole at the top of the piling. The special tough wood driver had been located and was in place on the steel shaft. A hole had been drilled through the driver, which was four feet high and about thirty inches in diameter. Ropes were attached to the top of the driver through eye holes carved into the wood. At the top of the thirty foot tall frame was a pulley through which the cable passed to the driver. The cable went through another pulley at the bottom of the scaffold, then to the winch on the back of one of the jungle logging trucks.

Lifting that chunk of wood up then letting it fall on the piling was a slow and tedious job. The rocky bottom of the river didn't make things any faster. The only way to release the winch was for a man to sit next to it with a hammer that with a blow to the proper anatomical site of the winch would allow the driver to fall. To make up for the slow motion process, the pile driving crew was at its task from daybreak to dark. I can still remember waking morning after morning to the sound of the slow thud, thud, thud. One day the hammer man was brought to the hospital on a litter. Somehow, which I never quite understood, he had become entangled in the cable suffering a broken tibia and fibula. Usually when things like that happened in those parts it was the work of spirits, moonshine rice whiskey. I put on a long leg cast and within a few days I saw him again at his post perched on the

Apee (shirtless) working on the wooden approaches to the bridge.

back of the truck with the hammer, so the process of coaxing the pilings the two meters into the rocky river bottom continued.

JUNGLE PROBLEMS

Kamnan Tun found me in the hospital one morning at a time I thought everything was going along well. One of the basic laws of the jungle is that when things seem to be going well, they aren't. He explained the problem. Someone had told the Nai Amphur that the Kamnan and I were playing around and didn't really intend to build a bridge. From the Kamnan's record of shrewd dealings in that area, the story was probably believable from the Nai Amphur's standpoint. I found out later that the locals thought it very strange that a doctor would be building a bridge. Anyway the Kamnan had been called in and queried about that rumor. Now he wanted me to go over to the Amphur office and reassure the Nai Amphur that we really meant business. I promptly went to do my duty and invited the Nai Amphur to come over and see for himself our progress. He accepted the invitation and the following Sunday afternoon, he showed up at our house for a visit.

The Nai Amphur looked over the progress of the bridge construction and the stockpile of pilings that the Kamnan had as well as the progress of the pile driving. We then went to our house to have a chat and something to drink. While we were seated in the living room, the children's pet civet cat (something akin to and having similar habits to a raccoon) slipped along the wall and behind the sofa where the Nai Amphur was seated. For some reason he bit the Nai Amphur on the heel, which gave him quite a fright. We quickly explained what had happened and that seemed to calm the situation, but before I knew it the critter had slipped around again to bite him the second time. That brought our little tea time to a closure. The next time I met the Nai Amphur, he laughed about the event, so I guess there were no hard feelings. At least there was no more issue about our intentions toward the completion of the bridge.

The next crisis came when the approaches were about three fourths complete and we were erecting the scaffolding that would support the steel span as it was being assembled. Apee had been hired by the Kamnan as the foreman of his section of bridge. Apee was a Muslim of Indian descent who had married a local Karen woman. He had worked for the mission at times and his little son, Ah-nin, was a frequent visitor to our home to play with our Lloyd and Andy. Apee was very strong and well versed in jungle skills especially logging and wood working so he was ideal for the job. At some time in the middle of the construction when I happened to be gone from the hospital for a few days, Apee's wife, Mashwe, appeared at the hospital in labor. The baby was delivered safely, but a postpartum hemorrhage tragically claimed the mother's life. Of course this was a terrific blow for Apee. For some reason he was not on good terms with his in-laws who lived a few hundred yards from the hospital, so they did not take any responsibility for the motherless newborn. For the first six months of his life, the nurses looked after the poor little waif. Apee would come now and then to check on him.

Apee's wife's death is not the crisis I intended to tell about as it didn't directly concern the bridge. One day I met Apee who woefully

Scaffolding being prepared for the center span. Hlaing standing on scaffolding made from betel nut trees.

Moving the 80 foot long double rail bottom tension member into place.

told me that the Kamnan was refusing to pay him his wages. That immediately angered me since we had been friends since first arriving in Sangklaburi and I felt guilty for not being present when his wife came to deliver. The Kamnan explained things to me in such a way as I couldn't understand, so I finally told him that I would not do any more work on the bridge until Apee had been paid his wages. I had been interested in the "Death Railway" and read many books about that saga of WWII. It often seemed that the ghosts of the one hundred thousand Allied prisoners and conscripted Asians who had lost their lives in that oppressive ordeal hung about wanting redress for their grievances. I didn't want oppression in this venture for I had come to see the bridge as a possible monument to those poor souls. The British and Dutch had their beautiful and well kept war cemetery in Kanchanaburi, but the conscripted Asians (Burmese, Indian and Malaysian) had been buried and forgotten in mass graves throughout the jungle just where they fell as victims of cholera epidemics, malaria and other diseases that preyed on chronically malnourished and overlooked prisoners.

Tension hung in the air for a few days then Apee came by and told me that he had been paid. I called my men back and work resumed. By

Upper steel structure being assembled.

A worker "walking" up one of the steel uprights. No ladders were used in constructing the 20 foot tall bridge.

this time the pilings at each end of the steel span were completed and the heavy timber bridge support was bolted into place. Two rows of three pilings with an extra piling at each end would support the steel span. The heavy crossbraces were bolted into place on the pilings. Rafts from the upriver logging operations could break away and come down upon the supports, so we wanted it as strong as possible.

ASSEMBLING THE STEEL SPAN

When the Kamnan's crew completed the bridge decking up to the center span, we had our scaffold ready so as to begin reassembling the steel. The first chore was to lay the tension member (the bottom steel rails) of the trusses in place and bolt the joint plates between them then connect the two tension members with the cross pieces which would hold up the floor of the bridge. Nai Chert and Nai Hlaing, with the help of others, moved the rails into place and had that chore completed in short order. I had picked up some small wheeled trolleys from Bangkok that made the chore very easy.

Getting the steel up in the air was the tricky part. The only means of lifting anything was the winch on the front of our jungle truck. After a bit of talking amongst ourselves, we decided on a method. The steel uprights were twenty feet long, so a bit cumbersome to lift upright. The first set of uprights were attached to the bottom joint plate with one bolt, which would allow them to swivel upward. The top joint plates were then attached and the cross member bolted in place, thus forming an inverted U. The old truck was driven up on the approach in front of an A frame scaffold. The winch cable was run through a pulley attached to the A frame scaffold then the cable was attached to the middle of the steel cross member. The steel was then lifted enough to attach the first set of upright braces.

Getting that first set of steel uprights in place and just right for the lifting was a time consuming chore. Nai Hlaing seemed to be the only one who understood just how the process would work. He was trying to explain to his men, but nothing was falling into place. She Shoe, our mission maintenance man, happened by at that time and was standing by the truck watching. After a while he began to talk. The confusion of the situation reminded him of the Old Testament story of the tower of

Completed bridge in 1977.

Completed bridge with Nai Chert the village blacksmith (with hat) and Nai Hlaing the carpenter.

Babel. Working on the bridge that day was someone from about every language group in the area, at least a half dozen. A few minutes later as I was sitting in the truck waiting to operate the winch, Nai Hlaing came over and with a bit of disgust in his voice informed me in his broken Thai that he had used every language he knew and still could not get the men to do the right thing. He could speak Mon, Burmese, Thai and a bit of Karen. I then went over and, with a bit of encouragement, helped get the steel lined up just right.

The winch then slowly lifted the steel to the upright position and the uprights and braces were bolted into place without too much trouble. To me that was cause for a bit of celebration for the hardest part was completed. The pulley was moved from the A frame to the steel cross member and the next day the second set of uprights with their braces were raised up. The bridge rapidly took shape, but much of the steel bracing had to be manhandled into place with drilling of many rails as they were put in place.

As the bridge took shape, I could sense a different attitude in Nai Hlaing and Nai Chert. It seemed that there was more of a sparkle in their demeanor and a sense of pride as they realized the center span was becoming a reality. I will have to confess that I too was proud of what had been accomplished by the village blacksmith and the local carpenter.

In the history of the Mon, there had been an advanced culture, but now there was little left of it. They had "had their turn" as a friend of mine once said of such cultures. To be among the Mon was to feel that there was still something special that carried over from that past. They were a tall, thin people who carried themselves with dignity, and so it was with Nai Hlaing. He was also a craftsman who would not do anything that he could not be proud of. So I could sense in his changing attitude the sense of pride of workmanship as well as of being part of something that would be of significance in our jungle community.

I particularly noticed that in Nai Hlaing for we had been involved in some other projects that were not successful. One of my schemes had been to make a flow under water wheel that would power a pump lifting water from our rapidly flowing little river up the bank for irrigation purposes. It was composed of two large bamboo rafts situated in an A that would funnel water to the wheel situated down stream at

Ten years later. Olivia and village health team in ox cart. Hospital crew on ground with Dr. Phil in center, Nancy and I on far right.

the apex. Hlaing had been engaged for the project. There were many modifications such as the addition of flywheels to smooth the working of the piston pump. The contraption made a lot of noise with its whirling wheels but never produced the necessary flow of water. Finally one day Nai Hlaing asked me a question that seemed loaded with more insinuations, accusations and suspicions than I can ever remember in a question. He simply asked in his toneless Thai (which changed the word for Doctor to black cooking pot) "Doctor, have you ever made one of these before?" That same night a flash flood came down our little river and washed the whole thing away. A few weeks later someone told me of some old cart wheels, remnants of the water wheel, seen down river. Nai Hlaing was glad that I didn't pursue that any further.

The steel work of the bridge had been mostly completed when I had to make a quick trip to Bangkok for more supplies, mostly drill bits. On my return I was surprised to find that the scaffolding had been removed from under the bridge. Many more bolts were needed in certain places and I had intended a final inspection before the bridge was

The original crew of the hospital at its reopening in 1974.

John and Josie looking over a chart.

left free standing. I had never been on top of the bridge for inspection as the workers had never produced a ladder. The workers didn't need one as they "walked" up the twenty foot vertical rails as a monkey would. Naturally I did not have that talent so the top of the bridge was never seen by me, but I trusted my two foremen. The Kamnan needed his lumber and posts that made up our scaffolding so that was the reason for its removal. Nai Hlaing proudly informed me that the bridge didn't sag an inch when the scaffold was removed.

As mentioned he had never worked with steel before.

DISAPPOINTMENT

The bridge was nearing completion when our family left for a week or so to attend the annual mission conference. On return I was informed that the bridge had been completed and the dedication ceremony by the government had been performed. The ceremony was not such an important event, but when one is in such an isolated and remote place, little events like that take on a special significance. I made my way over to see the completed project and was a little dismayed

One of Olivia's village health scenes.

Arriving in Three Pagoda Pass for a village clinic. The rock path is the old service road for the Death Railroad.

The Freemans on an outing to Japanese Well (note water in foreground). This is midway point between Sangklaburi and Three Pagoda Pass. The well was dug by the Japanese as they built the railroad.

A fuzzy aerial view of the bridge with mission in the background. The Hosptial is nearer the river.

The newly completed church in Sangklaburi in 1977.

to see hanging on the steel bridge a sign that read "Public Bridge No. 2." Though I had not mentioned it to the government officials, I had hoped to call it"Friendship Bridge" in memory of the many Asians who had died on the "Death Railway."

There was a very large post blocking each end of the approaches to the bridge, preventing vehicles other than motorcycles from passing over the bridge. The Kamnan explained to me that under the contract he must guarantee the bridge for one year so the posts insured that there would be no damage from a heavy vehicle. No one told me life in the jungle would be easy.

TEN YEARS LATER

In 1983 I traveled to Sangklaburi in an air-conditioned van over a paved road to visit the little hospital that we had helped reopen in 1974. In the intervening ten years, plenty had changed in what had then been one of the most remote places of Thailand. The communist insurgents that were only a days walk from us had abandoned their efforts by surrendering to the government in an amnesty agreement. When we left a few months after completion of the bridge, Thailand was still under a cloud of gloom and pessimism from the threat of the spread of communism. While we were there, I did all I could to prepare the hospital to continue to serve without a missionary doctor and without outside help if it should come to that.

It didn't come to that. Dr. Phil McDaniel and his family had been there several years by the time of my visit and he was ideally suited for the expanding work of the hospital. Both his father and grandfather had been Presbyterian medical missionaries in Thailand. His father Dr. Ed was a pioneer of family planning in Thailand and had given me training in that area. He was a regular visitor to the hospital to give Phil relief and to consult in Ob-Gyn as well as family planning. With the new roads, the hospital was overrunning with patients and plenty busy.

The Burmese regime had increased their brutality resulting in thousands of refugees from that sad country meagerly existing in the nearby jungles who depended so much on the little hospital for it was still the only place surgery services were available in that area. Burmese refugees had trickled through when we had been there, so I had gained and earful about the misery of the people of Burma.

Naturally I walked over to have a look at the bridge. Some children crossed on their way home from school then an ox cart rattled the now loose boards of the one way bridge. Before I left we had traded and old jungle truck for an oxcart to be used for the village health work. It would be very inexpensive to operate. Transmissions, brakes, etc. did not have to be repaired on an ox cart, nor did it need diesel, which at that time was very expensive. Olivia had continued to use that ox cart as the village health work expanded. She and he team crossed the bridge many times on her way to the villages in the years since we left.

Olivia was proud of what had been accomplished in the village health program. According to her not one child under five years of age who was a regular attendee of her clinics had died in the years since the program had started. That was quite a record for that malaria-infested part of the world where almost every child had a belly full of worms. Then I thought of Josie Falla, the spunky little Australian Baptist missionary nurse who had the idea of the village health clinics in the first place.

We met Josie when we first went to look at Sangklaburi and the hospital in February of 1974. She was overjoyed when we told her that we may join her in getting the medical work there restarted. She worked as hard as a dingo to get things going and about the time things were running smoothly, she had to return home because of health reasons. She would be pleased at what her vision had brought forth. I offered a prayer of thanks for the many bridge builders that I had known in the jungles of Sangklaburi.

POST SCRIPT

Public Bridge #2 had served its purpose for ten years when the hydroelectric dam ten kilometers down river was completed. The village of Sangklaburi, including the mission, was moved to a new location to avoid the flooding. The bridge now sits at the bottom of the lake with the very top visible when the water is very low.

CAMBODIA CONNECTION

JUNGLE FEVER

Sorn and I were in the middle of the medical ward of the ANS(Army Nationale Sihanouk) field hospital. We were at the bedside of a young man recovering from a severe bout of cerebral malaria. This illness, he had said, was caused by Plasmodium falciparum, the killer variety common in the forested area of Northwest Cambodia where we were located. As I talked with Sorn, the chief medical worker of the ward, I was concerned with two things; his proficiency as a medical worker and diseases important to this part of Cambodia. Malaria, the most important disease in this area and the number-one killer, was the topic of our conversation. However I couldn't help monitoring the sights and sounds around me. The steady monsoon rain falling softly on the woven grass roof brought back old memories. On the next bed over, a patient's family eating their midday rice meal, sat huddled together. The patient slept oblivious to the activities on the foot of his bed. Under the bed a couple of scrawny chickens scratched about on the packed earth floor. Under another bed, a thin hungry-looking dog patiently watched the eating, hoping for a left-over morsel. Across the ward several squealing children scampered in and out of the doorless building.

Just as I was moving to get out from under a small leak, my thoughts focused on Sorn's words. "Our treatment for malaria here is to give tetracycline and quinine three times a day for a week." This drug combination for the treatment of malaria had a special significance to me. Over and over during the months of September and October on this trip I heard that same reply in response to the question, "What is your treatment of falciparum malaria?"

The early Fall of 1991 had an air of expectancy for Cambodians and Cambodia watchers. Several factors relating to the economic collapse of communism and socialism had put a peaceful settlement of the war-torn and famished Cambodia within grasp. Vietnam had become an economic basket case and was very desirous of captalist investments. The Red Chinese support of the Kymer Rouge had slowed to a trickle. Pol Pot, the Kymer Rouge leader, had grown rich from gem-mining concessions in the Cardamon mountains in Southwest Cambodia. Hopefully, he would be more interested in his financial holding across the border in Thailand than in trying to rule Cambodia again. The political savvy of Prince Norodom Sihanouk had gained him center stage in the peace negotiations. He had managed to get the three resistance factions and the Cambodian government together at the peace table.

At this time our International Medical Corps medical assessment team arrived to take a look at the medical programs of the two Cambodian non-communist resistance groups. Our job was to look at the situation and make recommendations for redirecting the military supported medical program to one geared to meeting the needs of the civilian populations in their areas.

Malaria will continue to be a problem long after peace is established. Some malaria such as the vivax variety is easily treated but falciparum often produces a very severe illness which may result in death. During our eight years in Thailand I had treated many people with malaria, but one case still is vivid in my memory. In 1980-81, we were back in Thailand working with the Cambodian refugees. During that time our mission had asked us to go to the Kwai River Christian Hospital to relieve Dr. Phil McDaniel for his annual vacation. Since we had worked there (1974-77) previously, I was eager to go and see the place and the many old friends. After arrival in Sangklaburi, Phil gave me a quick summary of the patients in the hospital. "The main problem," he said, "is the pregnant woman with cerebral malaria." She had not been responding to the medications.

For the next three days, this little Karen mother remained unconscious and at the point of death. Blood transfusions and perhaps a change in the medical treatment kept her alive. Only after a stillborn delivery did she begin to show signs of improvement. More transfusions and about two more weeks passed before she was able to leave the hospital. The morning of discharge, the husband had their two little children together with the mother. She was sitting up with the reed bed mat rolled up and the few simple possessions tied in a pakama (a 3 ft. by 5 ft. loincloth used by the men). For this simple hilltribe family, there was a silent but palpable rejoicing that this mother and wife was going home.

From the doorway of our small twelve-bed jungle hospital, I watched as the little family walked down the lane. The three-year old was carried by the father and the five-year old held to the mother's hand. Due to the mother's weakened condition, they would stop many times before reaching their small bamboo house in the distant village. A pig, a few chickens and a dog probably awaited their return. Soon, she would be cooking rice over the fire in her kitchen again. The fire would be made on a dirt box in the middle of the floor and the ricepot held up by three or four rocks. Malaria would continue to stalk this jungle family, but for the moment the fire of love would continue to burn.

This summer, July '91, I had another occasion to visit the Kwai River Christian Hospital. Nancy, Krista and I had been to Jonlyn's graduation from Woodstock School in India. Jonlyn had spent her last two years of high school as an exchange student there in that international boarding school. Naturally, Krista and Jonlyn wanted to visit the land of their birth, so we stopped in Bangkok for a week. While visiting the hospital on the Kwai I discussed old times and acquaintnaces with Phil. Since malaria was still a major problem, that subject came up. They too were using the tetracycline and quinine combination for the treatment of severe malaria.

Toward the end of the IMC survey I had the opportunity to visit the Maesariang Christian Hospital in North Thailand. That is a small sister hospital to the one in Kanchanaburi on the River Kwai. Dr. Bina Sawyer wanted me to visit with the hope that I would come to replace her when she retired. Since the location is in a forested area near the Burmese border, malaria had become an increasing problem there in recent years. For their severe malaria, they were using the same drug combination as in the other areas I had visited.

So here in 1991 the drug combination of tetracycline and quinine was being used along the Thai-Burmese, the Thai-Cambodian borders as well as other places to treat severe malaria. This treatment was saving the lives of thousands of poor rural villagers every year.

To understand the significance to me of that malaria treatment we must drop back ten years to Kamput, a Cambodian refugee camp in the Cardamon Mountains just inside Southeast Thailand. In 1979 missionary friends of ours, Dan and Fan Cobb, discovered some destitute Cambodians in this area and began a relief effort to help them. The Cambodians had managed to escape the murderous regime of Pol Pot's Kymer Rouge as the invading Vietnamese army came in to install their own puppet government in Cambodia. These malnourished and malaria-infected refugees kept pouring across the border, so that by the time we arrived in 1980 there were numerous United Nations administered refugee camps established.

Kamput was located about 100 kilometers north of Chantaburi which is the gem-polishing capital of Southeast Asia. The cardamon Mountains to the East of Chantaburi are famous for gem-mining, especially rubies. Those same mountains are famous among malariologists for something else. The area just inside Cambodia is the epicenter of resistant falciparum malaria. The resistant to chloroquine started there and has spread over the world. In 1979, the malnourished Cambodians seeking to escape their communist-ravaged country had to traverse the malaria-infested Cardamon Mountains to get across the border. It was soon discovered that the malaria they brought with them was totally resistant to the newer antimalarial Fansidar. Fansidar was a drug developed to treat chloroquine-resistant falciparum malaria and had worked like a charm for over ten years but was useless in 1979 in that area.

When we arrived in the Spring of 1980, the malaria problem was still serious. Refugees, especially children, were dying daily from malaria. I was assigned the job of medical coordinator for the Kamput Refugee camp. Within a few days, I was informed that there would be a meeting in the camp of the malaria specialists from Bangkok. Later specialists from the World Health Organization came. Assistance was then requested from the malaria division at the Communicable Disease Center in Atlanta. We had no more gotten settled in the work there when Dr. Ken Campbell arrived from the CDC.

Kent came with an idea for the treatment of malaria as well as veins full of adrenalin, for he was a lean, lank marathoner. As is usual of his type, he was in a powerful hurry to get a study going to test his idea. I have never figured out whether Kent ran so he could enjoy that rush of adrenalin or ran in order to use up his excess energy. One thing I was sure of was that he had never worked in the jungle where life was

Meeting in Kamput with malaria experts from Bangkok. Dr. Kent Campbell at the far end of the table with arms crossed.

Cambodian malaria study workers.

Malaria study ward.

John with two Cambodian helpers.

slow. Several refugee camps were to conduct the test simultaneously. Kent chided me for being so slow to get the study going. The other camps were ready to go, so he said. I had been working trying to get the study started at Kamput, but life in the jungle is slow. It was slow especially since we had an ex-navy commander as the head nurse of the hospital. She was accustomed to getting her way and, moreover, she was on the side of the majority of refugee workers who thought it was wrong to "experiment on the poor Cambodian refugees...after all, they had suffered enough, etc." People were dying every day, so my attitude was more pragmatic. We needed, desperately, an effective malaria treatment. However since our camp medical policies were arrived at democratically, it was hard to organize for the study. Persistence finally paid off. It also gained me some persistent enemies. We set aside a special ward to be used for the study and trained the special-duty health workers for the work.

As it turned out, the "anti-experiment" forces prevailed in all the other camps, so Kamput was the sole site of the study, The study showed conclusively that tetracycline and quinine three times a day for a week was effective in treating resistant falciparum malaria. This then became the standard treatment for that type of malaria in all of the camps.

Since that time, a newer antimalarial, mefloquine, was introduced for resistant malaria. Now in the Cardamon Mountain area fifty percent of the malaria is resistant to that drug, but the combination tetracycline and quine is still effective. Kent's idea of the combined treatment proved to be a bright star in the treatment of falciparum malaria. Admittedly my part in the study, that of facilitator, was small but the study did get done in spite of the stiff opposition, and it has brought healing to thousands of poor villagers in malarious areas. But this is only part of the story.

A CASE OF COMPLICATED PNEUMONIA

It was Sunday morning, October 6, 1991, at the Aranchai Hotel three kilometers east of Aranyaprathet and about three kilometers from Poiphet, Cambodia which is the main border crossing between Thailand and Cambodia. I was glancing over yesterday's Nation while eating breakfast in the open sala resturant facing the highway. There was a constant stream of tour buses loaded with Thai tourists heading toward the border. A market with Vietnamese and Cambodian goods for sale had recently sprung up at the border as a result of the peace process. The market had grown so fast there was not time for proper development so it was in a muddy field and called the Mud Market of Aranyaprathet. Tourists from as far away as Bangkok came on weekends and rented boots to wade through the muddy stalls.

An article on the editorial page "Mourning the Death of Thai Democracy" caught my eye and took my mind off the caravan of passing buses. I had not thought much about the recent headlines stating that the Thai military government would not tolerate protests or demonstrations during the upcoming World Bank meeting in Bangkok. The Bank meetings would be in progress on October 13th. The lead editorial article told about the modern Thai struggle for democracy beginning with the October 13, 1973, student uprising. University students at that time were protesting the corrupt dictators then in power. As a result of the bloody suppression by the military and police, the Thai people appealed to the King to intervene. King Bhumipol did make what was an unusual appeal to the three dictators who promptly left the country.

I remembered that October 13th very vividly. We were at that time living in Bangkla, one hundred kilometers east of Bangkok where I was working in the Bangkla Baptist Hospital. Our "lukliang"(Thai, meaning to take to raise) Boonsong needed to go to Bangkok to see an ear specialist. Boonsong, fourteen at the time, had come to live with us in order to attend school. His appointment with the ear specialist was on October 13th. No Thai wants to travel alone so he asked if Lloyd, then six years old, could go with him. We had no idea of any trouble, so we allowed Lloyd to go along. Just before noon that day news came over the radio of rioting and killing in Bangkok. Rumors magnified the problem of course. Boonsong and Lloyd would be in the same location as the trouble There was nothing we could do but pray and wait. After what seem an eternity Boonsong and Lloyd arrived on the five o'clock bus. They acted as if nothing had happened except a bus ride to Bangkok.

Such is the respect and love the Thai people feel for their king that they turn confidently to him in a crisis. The leaders, corrupt and powerful as they were, had no choice but to respect the wishes of the king as well and leave the country. I never saw the king, but during the dark days at Kamput events took place that would affect the life of this beloved king.

Dr. Amporn was the medical coordinator of the Thai Red Cross team at Kamput at the same time as my term there. This delightful and energetic professor of infectious disease at Chulalongkorn University became a good friend of ours. She thought often of ways to make our life there a bit more pleasant. Just before Lloyd and Andrew went to Woodstock, she invited us to a dinner in their honor. Often she brought gifts for Krista and Jonlyn.

Many of the Cambodian refugees had respiratory infections that did not respond to the usual antibiotic treatment. This reminded me of a type of atypical pneumonia, usually not severe, that is caused by the bacteria Mycoplasma pneumoniae. One morning at our daily medical conference I mentioned that the epidemic of respiratory disease in the camp may be due to Mycoplasma. Dr. Amporn thought it was doubtful since to her knowledge this infection had never been reported in Thailand. Since she was the specialist in infectious disease, I deferred to her opinion. A few days later Dr. Amporn completed her tour there and went back to her duties in Bangkok. Less than a week later a note from her arrived. She had been reading and became convinced also that our epidemic was indeed due to Mycoplasma pneumoniae. She asked that I help her do a study to document the epidemic.

By this time I was caught in a crossfire of troubles. It didn't take long to accept a job that would get me out of the line of fire. The mission allowed me to spend the last several months helping Dr. Amporn with the Mycoplasma study. I spent my time tracking patients and collecting blood samples and clinical data. Dr. Amporn was busy setting up the first laboratory in Thailand to study this fastidious bacteria. By the end of my contract we had completed our studies. Several papers were written and Dr. Amporn was established as the authority on Mycoplasma pneumoniae infections in Thailand. She continued her investigations for several more years.

Three years later while working in Saudi Arabia, I returned to Bangkok for a medical meeting. While there, I called Dr. Amporn to say hello. She wanted to tell me "the rest of the story" so we met for lunch. The year before, King Bhumipol had taken ill. His condition deteriorated to the point the doctors were very concerned, since he was not responding to any of the antibiotics. Eventually Dr. Amporn was called for consultation. The king was gravely ill with pericarditis, a complication of an infectious process. After her examination, Dr. Amporn took a blood sample for tests. The test done in her lab confirmed her suspicion of Mycoplasma pneumonia infection which was complicated by pericarditis. The king began his recovery when the proper antibiotics were prescribed. Mycoplasma infection is peculiar in that it responds to only two antibiotics.

We had noticed a variety of complications of Mycoplasma infection in Kamput. One of our papers recounted the various manifestations of the infection as seen in Kamput. The review of the literature about this subject had helped prepare Dr. Amporn for that moment in the life of the King who was so loved by his people. Dr. Amporn knew of my trouble at Kamput and wanted me to know that there was indeed a silver lining to that dark cloud I had been under while at Kamput.

DARK DAYS

In late 1979, the world's attention was focused on the tragedy occuring in Cambodia. When the Vietnamese invaded, the regime of Pol Pot was thrown into turmoil. In the confusion, hundreds of thousands of starving and terrified Cambodians seized the opportunity to flee. Thousands died or were killed in their struggle to find freedom across the border in Thailand. The survivors who arrived at the numerous refugee camps along the border were often at the point of death.

Among those responding to the immediate crisis were doctors and staff from the three small Baptist hospitals in Thailand. The Baptists were given responsibility for the hospital in the Kamput refugee camp.

For me, adjusting to life and medical practice in the States had been difficult after seven years of work among the village people of Thailand. Disease patterns were very different, but most important was the sense of satisfaction derived from treating the diseases of the villagers, most of which they had no control over. It had been hard for me to develop sympathy for the self-induced American diseases; smoking-related, alcohol, overeating, sexually-related, etc. Moreover, I had developed a fondness for rural life and for rural health development. To me, it was a challenge to make the rural areas healthier places to live so there would not be the need for migration to the dehumanizing, crowded cities. Picture the twelve-year-old boy lazily napping on the back of a grazing water buffalo; then compare his cousin in polluted Bangkok selling flower garlands in the rush-hour traffic, dodging cars in his attempt to help earn a living. My yearning heart jumped at the opportunity to return to work in Thailand in a Cambodian refugee camp. Hopefully this would later lead to continued work in rural Thailand.

In the Spring of 1980, Nancy and I and our children, Lloyd, Andrew, Krista and Jonlyn were off to Thailand again. Immediately on arriving, we were taken to the little market village of Tapsai, 100 kilometers north of Chantaburi. I was informed that my job would be medical coordinator of the Kamput refugee camp located east of Tapsai an hour's drive and about ten kilometers from the Cambodian border. Part of my job was seeing that all ran smoothly among the

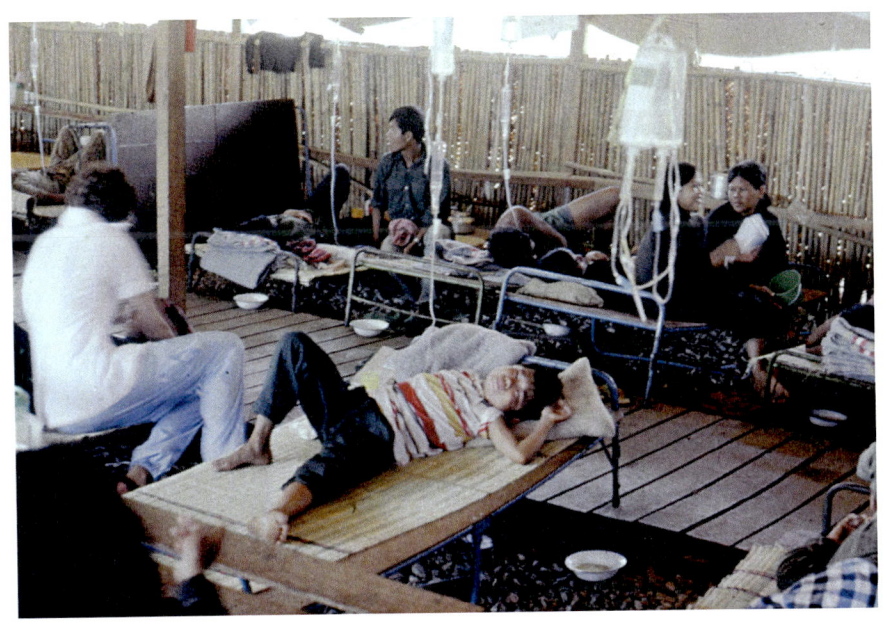

Kamput hospital ward.

Kamput scene.

various groups who had responsibility for various medical activities in the camp. The Thai Red Cross was in charge of the surgery; Concern (Irish) was doing the public health; another group was in charge of camp sanitation. Jamie Robertson, an independent, appeared from somewhere to do dental work. His skill at making dental partial plates restored the traditional smile of many young Cambodian girls.

The rest of the day was occupied by hospital rounds, teaching interpreters and medical workers and working in out-patient clinics. The out-patient clinics were composed of a crude table and stools covered by a woven grass roof and surrounded by walls three feet high. Several people were usually hovering around, looking and listening over those little partitions. Frequently, we had to interrupt our exam while the patient answered the comments of interested bystanders.

By the time we arrived, the operation was fairly well organized, but much needed to be done. A crowded refugee camp is an ideal environment for epidemics. An illness rapidly spreads to every one in the camp. However the greatest burden of a situation like that was the daily contact with personal tragedies. Kamput camp was composed of thousands of faces all covering a story of horror, suffering, and family disruptions. The most striking example of this in our camp was that of the "Unaccompanied Minors." This was a term created especially for the Cambodian Crisis. These were children ten to fourteen years age, mostly boys, who had been forcibly taken from their families and placed in Pol Pot's reindoctrination schools. Most of these children hadn't seen their families in two to three years when the Vietnamese invaded and threw the country into further chaos. In the confusion, the cadre of the schools simply threw open the doors and told the students to run. Hundreds of these bewildered children followed the crowds into Thailand. We had a large secion of our camp for these children who did not know where their parents were or if they were alive. I would walk throught this section now and then and talked to some of the children. At any mention or question of their families the boys would simply turn their heads and look silently into space. No tears, just a sad silent stare.

Nancy's job was no small task either. She managed in short order to make the Tapsi house into a home. It was more like a boarding house. We had a cook borrowed from Dr. Bina Sawyer in Maesariang. Sawang could produce both a smile and a meal for any number in a minute. Soon there were several others living in the house, a couple of YWAM (Youth with a Mission), the cook and Philip Harris, my nephew who came to help with food distribution.

We had no more arrived when Nancy started on the education problem. Krista and Jonlyn would be taught at home by Nancy using the Calvert program. Lloyd and Andrew would need to go to a boarding school. After some discussion with the boys, the Christian international boarding school in the foothills of the Indian Himalayas was chosen. I couldn't be spared, so Nancy had to take them to Woodstock School. And that trip turned out to be a rather troublesome experience for Nancy. By the end of the year they had come to like the school. When Nancy returned, the Calvert home school began. There were usually a few neighbor children peering in the window during the classes.

A good thing about Tapsai was the poor family across the street. They had about ten children, mostly girls, Soon Krista, Jonlyn and the neighbor girls were all like "penong" (brothers and sisters) and they filled the days with play.

Other than the poor neighbor with the ten children and the close proximity to Kamput there is not much good to say about Tapsai. It was the noisest place we have ever lived. There were at least three major dog fights each night just outside our window. At four AM the blacksmith who lived in our backyard began beating on his anvil shaping the large knives he made for a living. Before dawn each day the ice shop just down the street announced its opening by turning on a monster ice crusher. The racuous sound of grinding ice permeated the market place, and I wondered each morning how the Thai could use so much crushed ice. The houses were all close enough that we could hear the neighbors' midnight arguments when the husbands would come in drunk. At least once a month a traveling movie would set up in the adjacent vacant lot. The amplifers were aimed at the village for advertisement. The deafening noise went on all night as movie after movie was projected until daybreak when the sleepy families rolled up their mats and trudged back to their homes.

All of these inconveniences and primitive living, including squat toilets and cold pour baths, were tolerated well enough since we felt we were helping those in need. However about six months into the work, relationships within our mission group began to fall apart. Things grew progressively worse, so I was offered a position at a Hmong refugee camp in North Thailand. I elected to stay in Kamput to help with another medical study (more about this later). Reaction to what developed led me to a new low of frustration and even bitterness. What the problem was and whose fault it was is part of the past and nothing is gained by dwellng on such matters. But looking back on those days it seems that they were some of the darkest days of my life. Hopes of further work in Thailand had faded. The type of work that I loved the most was not to come to pass. A sense of personal failure pervaded my thoughts and lingered even into future years. We made up our minds to complete the one year contract at Kamput and return to the States.

So many different problems developed that it seemed to Nancy and me that the trip to Thailand had been a mistake. The results of the malaria study though was a small comfort at the time. Seeing the benefits of that malaria study on this trip in 1991 along with what I had learned on another trip to Thailand a few years learlier painted that dark year with a little brighter color.

AN ANSWERED PRAYER

Thursday evening October 17, 1991, was the last in Bangkok for the IMC trip. Our survey of the Cambodian resistance medical programs was complete and the final meeting over. I asked Jean Paul Heldt, our team leader, if he wanted to go with me for one last visit with Eiam. We set off walking the mile or two down Wireless Road toward the Bangkok Nursing Home (hospital) where Eiam was a staff nurse.

Bangkok had been cleaned up for the World Bank Meeting, but the street vendors were returning to the sidewalks. Traffic at this time was heavy and moving at its usual crawl. Finally we turned into Convent Road and then to the Nursing Home. Fortunately Eiam was off duty so we three walked to the "Dark Window Restaurant" to get dinner and catch up on the latest events in Eiam's life.

We had known Eiam since our first week in Thailand in 1970, when she came to work in our home. At that time she was fourteen years old with a fourth-grade education. The daughter of tenant farmers near Minburi on the outskirts of Bangkok, she had never seen the inside of a foreigner's home before. Eiam was typical of the rural Thai, shy, pleasant, diligent, with a ready smile, and she loved children. Lloyd and Andrew, at that time four and three years old were treated like little brothers. A year later on Father's Day Krista was born in the Bangkok Nursing Home. By that time Eiam was as one of the family. That Father's Day lingers clear in my memory. As I stood in the hospital looking at my present I thought that Krista was the prettiest baby I had ever seen. Nancy enjoyed that hospital stay more than any other so we were both glad that Eiam had a good job there now. She had just spent several years working in the Kwai River Hospital where she had been of tremendous help. Her father had recently died, so it was good that she could now be near her mother.

Eiam was still helping in our home when we decided to move to the jungles of Kanchanaburi to work in the Kwai River Christian Hospital. It was difficult for Eiam to leave her family and move to such a remote place, but she had come to love Nancy like a mother. She moved with us to the little mission station at the headwaters of the

Kwai River near the Burmese border.

Life there was a bit lonesome, so Eiam was a great comfort and help to Nancy. By then, we had four children. Jonlyn was only six months old when we moved there. The children's school was in our home with Nancy as the teacher. A tributary of the Kwai, the Rantee, was just in front of our house. With that situation, Eiam was a welcome help.

During the second year there, Eiam developed painful blisters in her mouth that wouldn't heal. Nancy went to the books and soon diagnosed pemphigus. The condition didn't respond to my simple treatment. Since pemphigus is a chronic and sometimes fatal condition, we soon took her to Bangkok to a dermatologist and left her there to live at home during treatment.

A few months went by without any word from Eiam. One day Nancy said that she was worried about Eiam and wanted to go see about her. We packed for the difficult and tedious trip through the jungle and down the river to Bangkok. The day after we arrived, we made our way out to Minburi and then to the village on the klong (canal) where Eiam lived. We finally found a long-tailed boat driver who knew the family. Soon we were gliding noisily past clusters of lotus in blossom and houses built alongside the klong. Here and there people were lowering their large square nets into the klong to catch small fish and shrimp. Finally we came to a simple little bamboo house with a woven grass roof. A child ran to notify Eiam's mother that farangs (white-faced foreigners) had arrived. Eiam's mother was thrilled to see us and took us into their humble home. There was an opening for a door and packed earth for a floor. Part of the house had a raised wooden platform for sleeping and sitting. Our eyes were immediately fixed on the barely recognizable Eiam lying on the platform. Painful blistering lesions in varying stages covered her mouth and other parts of her body. She was thin and emaciated, being unable to eat because of the painful sores in her mouth. The family money was gone so there was nothing to do but wait for the end.

When we arrived at the Dermatology Hospital in Bangkok we were introduced to a young Thai doctor who had just completed his dermatology residency in America. He confidently explained the tests needed and the treatment for pemphigus. After several weeks Eiam was on her road to recovery. A month or so later she was able to return to our home while she continued her medications.

At about this time we were approaching our last year before furlough. Because of continued rebel activity, including Thai communists, in our area as well as mission policy, it seemed that we would not be able to return after furlough to Thailand. Nancy was wondering how she could help Eiam.

It looked strange, this twenty-one year old young lady wearing a 6th grade school uniform. Eiam attended our Christian school in Sangklaburi where the students were simple hilltribe children, so she was readily accepted. I thought to myself that it took a lot of courage to do what she was doing, but she seemed happy learning with the children. Nancy arranged for Eiam to continue her study at a Christian boarding school not too far from Bangkok after our departure. She did very well in that school as well, and was in the top of her class academically.

The graduation ceremony for Samuk Academy was in June 1980, soon after we had arrived to work at Kamput. A beautiful sunny warm day was common at that time of the year in Thailand. Eiam was pretty in her cap and gown, especially when she posed with her bouquet of roses. The thrill in her heart as well as ours at this occasion was great. Her mother was able to be present to see the first person in her family get this far in school. It was only a tenth-grade school. Nancy was already making plans for the last two years of high school and even for a school where Eiam could study nursing. Later, she earned a nursing degree from Pyap University in Chiangmai.

As Jean Paul and I walked back from the Bangkok Nursing Home that night I thought again of that June graduation day. At that time there was no thought of the troubles and disappointment soon to come. Eiam had told us that day that she had often prayed that we would be able to come to her graduation.

Didn't Jesus say that faith even as small as a grain of mustard seed could move mountains? Is it not possible for the simple faith of one of God's little ones to move a person from place to place? Soon after that graduation I was to react with bitterness to my passage through troubled waters. Tonight I prayed that in any future time of difficulty there would be peace and serenity with the realization that perhaps God was again answering the prayer of faith of one of His little ones.

BREAD CAST ON THE WATERS....

This last morning in Bangkok found me awake early. Soon I was out on the street looking for a sidewalk vender selling "platong koo" (unsweetened Y-shaped doughnuts). The sky was still overcast from the thunder and lightening monsoon rain of the night before. This only contributed to my melancholy mood. I found the "platong koo," then sat nearby in a sidewalk coffee shop. The vendor was selling pastries as fast as they could come out of the large wok deep fryer to people hurrying to work. Behind him the early morning traffic was still a bit thin.

Suddenly this scene passed from my consciousness and I was in Maesariang, a city in the North near the Burmese border and just south of the Golden Triangle. Just before this current project came up, we had been asked to return to Thailand to take the place of Bina Sawyer in the Maesariang Christian Hospital. It was a small rural hospital with an active village health program serving the hilltribe people in that area, mostly Karen but some Lawa. It was just the kind of work that appealed to me. Nancy and I had already began to talk about going there to work, and the children were happy that we might return to Thailand.

Dr. Paul Harvey and Dr. Peter Elliot, two other members of our team had traveled on a weekend trip up to Maesariang to see the hospital and talk with Dr. Sawyer. There were plenty of needs in the area especially in the village health program. Nurse Kim Brown told of another need. AIDS had come to some of the hilltribe villages(not the Karen however). The adults in some villages had tested 50% positive for this virus in a recent survey. Hilltribe girls were often lured, kidnapped or sold by poor parents into prostitution which is a major industry in Thailand. Kim told of her plans for a special AIDS education and support program for the hilltribe people.

The needs were there, no doubt about that. However, after the trip, I had the distinct feeling that for the present, Maesariang was not the place for me. My hopes had been rekindled at the prospect of returning the the land I loved so much. And now the hope was gone. But this was not the first time for frustrated hopes. Then I thought of the situations on this trip that had revealed to me how the small deeds done even in the dark and troublesome times can bring hope and healing to many.

My thoughts returned again to Maesariang and a nurse named Amporn. She had worked for fifteen years in that hospital helping in various ways. Various ways, yes, because she was partially paralyzed. Amporn and I had worked together years before at the Bangkla Baptist Hospital. She was only about twenty-five when a car struck her down in Bangkok. For three months, she lay unconscious not expected to live. Nancy and I visited her soon after her accident. She lay unconscious struggling to breathe. At Nancy's prodding, I found her doctor and in our discussion suggested a tracheostomy.

We had just visited Amporn in Maesariang and found the most radiant personality that I had encountered on the whole trip. Her mind had recovered completely, but she needed a wheelchair to get around. She seemed overjoyed to see me after so many years, and then pointed to the scar on her neck and thanked me for the suggestion to the doctor that day. Her mother had, no doubt, told her later of our visit. I had completely forgotten the visit, but perhaps that simple deed had saved her life. For almost fifteen years she had counseled those hilltribe patients about the illnesses, medications, and about the redeeming power of Christ.

My coffee was gone, as well as the sack of "platong koo." Even the vendor had sold out and gone, but I was still seated, lost in thought. Our ambitions and high hopes often don't end the way we plan. More important are the small deeds we perform along the way, the "bread we cast on the water. . . "

"WHAT ARE YOU DOING HERE?"

I still remember the first time it was put to me back in 1976 while working in the Kwai River Christian Hospital. The Queen Mother and her daughter the King's sister were to visit Sangklaburi for the purpose of dedicating a new Border Patrol school located near the Hospital. I was told that my family would be expected to be at the reception, so Nancy and I dutifully gathered our four children and drove off in our jungle truck with a load of school teachers. On the way mud splashed over the front of my clothes, but it was too late to change. I expected to stand off in the distance and watch, but we were ushered into the receiving line as there was not a large crowd in that isolated place. So after the formalities of opening the school were completed the Queen Mother and her daughter went down the line. They stopped in front of Nancy and muddy me with our four barefoot children (with thongs) then the king's sister asked, "What are you doing here?"

The following letters written in 1993 while serving in the Christian Hospital in Maesariang describe what we were doing in the jungle of Thailand. Since the children were grown Nancy and I were alone making for a lonely situation. It was that which led me to write a letter each week, mostly for their sake, telling of events in the present as well as the past creating an image of the land where they had spent much of their youth.

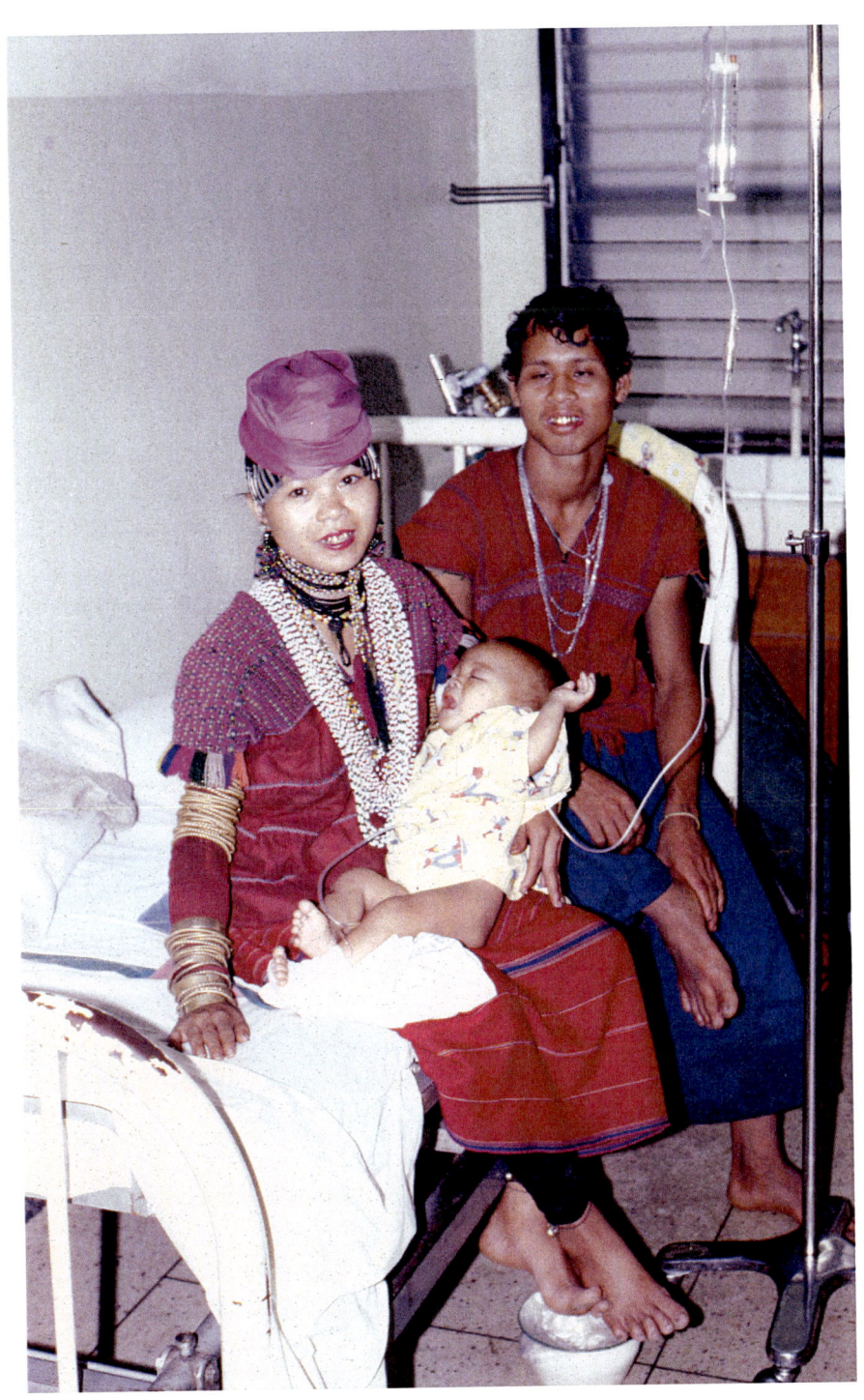

Tribal family in Maesariang Christian Hospital 1993.

March 9, 1993
A Trip to a Pwo Karen Village

    As the new medical director of the Maesariang Christian Hospital one of my duties is to oversee the village health program. So when the occasion arose, I chose to go on a trip with the mobile health team to some of the Pwo Karen villages in our area. The Pwo have been slower to turn from animism to Christianity and are a more backward group. Our mobile health team had been going to these villages for several years.

    That morning we left in a four-wheel drive truck for a two-hour drive which took us to a neat little village on the bank of a small river, the Omlo. This village was composed of Christians who, after becoming believers, relocated at this site because of the water and the good farm land which could be irrigated. They were encouraged to make the move by the missionaries who could see the advantages. Later the missionaries helped them construct an irrigation canal to their village, enabling them to plant year round crops of rice and soybeans. The houses in the village were constructed of bamboo with leaf roofs. Some houses were being replaced by lumber construction. I saw my first teak shake roof there. I thought that one of my antique froes would come in handy for the shake splitting. Pigs, chickens, ducks and children were happily running and playing together. Unmarried Karen girls wear home-woven long, white dresses decorated with red tassels and stitching. The boys have on red homemade pullover shirts.

    We didn't have a clinic in this village because it has a government health clinic. After eating our lunch we set out on foot for the village up the mountain. We followed the irrigation canal from the village. It was a refreshing walk beside the clear water, in the hot, dry season.

    Soon the fun ended as we began our climb upwards for a little over an hour's walk. Three hours later we (or I) struggled to the top of the mountain and into the village. This was the first time in several years I had made such a climb. In spite of the heart-pounding climb, it was a rather pretty walk through teak forests with scenic views of the surrounding "Karen Hills." We finally came to a small ravine where spring water was flowing out of a bamboo pipe. Two young girls from the village were completing their afternoon bath (fully clothed). We

A Karen woman with her bamboo water jars.

waited while they filled their large bamboo cylinder water containers; then we filled our bottles and had a nice cool drink. Another ten-minute walk and we were in Mae Louie.

Prechai, our medical worker, quickly found a house where we could sit in the shade & rest. It wasn't long before I was stretched out and only faintly aware of the continuous activity of the grunting pigs, roosters, chickens, goats, and children running about below the house. While we rested, a government malaria DDT spray team stopped at the house to chat before moving on to their next village. After about an hour I was finally able to get up and take a walk through the village.

The village of Mae Louie was a fairly typical Karen village except that it was mostly Christian. The houses were all of bamboo with the roofs made of a large tree leaf stitched together with bamboo strands. Some of the floors were made of sawed teak boards. The houses were all clustered together closely. Under each house were bamboo pens for the pigs, goats, chickens, and in some houses, cows. There were some water buffalo as well. All the animals are allowed to run free, so it was amazing to me that all of them find their proper home each night (I was assured that this was so). The place was a lot like a large barnyard.

After a supper of mostly rice flavored with a bit of fish paste mixed with garlic and chilies, we sat around in the little house and talked for about two hours. Several men from the village were there while we discussed the problems of their isolated existence. Their main problem was the water supply. The Government had given them pipe to bring water from a spring about a kilometer away, but it dries up in the dry season. They wanted me to look at another spring to see if water from it could be piped to the village. Their village site had been chosen by consulting spirits when the village was non-Christian. Spirits don't drink water so are not concerned with the distance to a water source.

In spite of the numerous animals, including dogs, the village was dead quiet during the night and, except for the frequent turns due to the hard floor, I got a pretty good night's rest. It seemed that all the roosters in the village signed up the night before to ensure that there would not be a moment's silence from four a.m. until dawn. Finally I heard other activity, so I decided to get up.

When I went outside I found that it wasn't dawn yet, just a full moon. Then I noticed a fire further up the village, so I decided to investigate.

Several men and boys were huddled around the fire watching two other men burn a whole goat on the fire. As it burned they scraped the skin with a bamboo stick. "An interesting way to cook a goat," I thought to myself. Not speaking Karen, I could only watch. After the goat was black all over it was laid on a bamboo mat and an incision made in the swollen abdomen. A dark green mushy substance spewed out hitting one of the men across the fire. A rather large heap of the "substance" spilled out on the mat. The two men then scooped up the "substance" and began massaging the goat with it. When the carcass was covered well, one of the men turned to me and explained that this was the method to keep the goat meat from stinking. In the glowing fire I recognized this man as the man of the house where I had slept. It then dawned on me that this goat was likely to be part of my breakfast. Needless to say there were a few thoughts going through my mind. They emptied the goat of its contents, took it off to wash it and then returned to complete the butchering process. We have whole hog barbecues in the South and I thought this was to be a whole goat roast. The skin was left on as it was a valuable source of protein.

My friend, Prechai and I then walked up to the spring that had been mentioned the night before. I was glad for the exercise for I needed all the help I could get to work up a good appetite. When we returned from the walk we were greeted with "It's time to eat." In the little house there was a pot of goat curry in the middle of the bowls of rice. The curry was the only dish, so there was no way out. The color of the curry matched the color of the abdominal "substance." These friendly Karens had butchered a goat for their guests, and there was nothing else to do but have some curry. What a pleasant surprise to taste a rather delicious meat curry! There was not a hint of goat flavor; they were right after all.

After Prechai, Myasa (our driver), and I finished our breakfast, the little Karen family with three children gathered around the table, a spot on the floor. Another surprise was to see each of them bow his head while the father offered thanks for the meal. This was a sight I was pleased to see each time I saw a Christian Karen family eat.

After breakfast, Prapa and Sriwan, our two nurses, gathered the team into another house and began the clinic. Prapa is a Karen Christian not long out of nursing school. It was a delight to see her joyfully taking care of the health needs of her people.

J. Freeman

March 1993
A Visit to Mae Pae

Three families of New Tribe missionaries live in the village of Mae Pae, which is about three hours drive from Maesariang. Last week Nancy and I went with one of the families to their village for a visit and as part of our orientation to the culture of this area. The last hour of our drive was a rather steep ascent to the Pwo Karen village of about 150 houses. When we arrived we found a rather friendly and gregarious people who seemed happy to have the American missionaries living among them. We looked around the primitive village, spent the night with the Beards, and then saw a few patients the next morning before going back home.

Today I met Scott, another of the missionaries, in the hospital. He told me about a death in the village since I had been there. I had been inquiring about the causes of death in the older population. Mya was a man of between fifty and sixty who had been ailing for several months and had been out of the village seeking a cure. He finally succumbed to abdominal pains, but before he died he dreamed that Gnaw had cast a spell on him. He recounted his dream to some of the villagers. When Mya died it was determined by the villagers that the cause of the death was the spell cast by Gnaw.

Usually in that village people are buried, but in the case of sorcery the body must be burned. Before the cremation the body must be examined to determine what has been put inside the abdomen by the spell. Scott watched as the men of the village performed a crude autopsy on the victim. A piece of liver was cut out. It smelled to one man like that of a cow. Another mass was removed and examined and when cut open contained a thick brown substance. After some discussion it was determined that sure enough the abdomen contained a mass placed there by the spell of a sorcerer, Mr. Gnaw.

Gnaw was confronted with the accusation which he flatly denied. Then the villagers told him that he must drink a special concoction which, if he were innocent he would live, but if guilty he would die. He consented and drank the water without effect on his health.

After the cremation of Mya, Scott found out that Gnaw had fled the village for fear of his life. The villagers had decided that he was guilty after all and would kill him. His wife had already died and all his children, except a ten-year-old daughter, were grown and married. He had taken his ten-year-old daughter and gone, it was said, to a far away village to live.

In different parts of the world people are in bondage to different evil spirits, but are the beliefs of the villagers of Mae Pae any worse than the bondage to drugs, pleasure, alcohol and the other gods that we worship?

J. Freeman

18 May 1993

Dear Friends,

The chronic cough, weight loss, and wasted facial muscles-since tuberculosis is common here, I was about to write some orders for TB tests when another thought came to mind. The order for an HIV test was written on the chart instead. An hour later the chart was back on my desk: HIV – positive.

Somsack was a 28-year-old truck driver from a distant town who happened to be in Maesariang, so he stopped in to get his cough checked. He had been to another hospital for tests, but they told him everything was all right. It is not the Thai custom to tell a patient when he tests positive for AIDS, but Somsack probably already suspected the reason for his weight loss.

He seemed to appreciate me telling him what the problem was. There was a wife and a two year old son at home. He would need to tell his wife, who was by this time most likely positive as well. Plans would need to be made for someone to raise the son. We talked as long as he wanted to; then I prayed with him that he would have strength and wisdom for the time of illness. I would never in all likelihood see Somsack again, a bright young man who had sacrificed so much for a moment of pleasure.

Later in the morning my nurse asked me if I thought that AIDS was God's punishment for sin. The Bible does tell us that the wages of sin is death, but I told her that I thought there was more than that. Jesus once said that those who offend one of these little ones deserves a millstone to be tied about their neck and tossed into the sea. Undisciplined sexual behavior leads to the birth of unwanted children. How many tens of thousands each year? These children grow up and live a lifetime filled with rejection, anger, frustration, and often rage. Who has the right to do that to another person? Perhaps AIDS is the millstone hung around the neck of those who are willing to offend the little ones. Of course there are the innocent ones who are affected as well.

I am proud of the compassionate way our nurses and staff take care of the AIDS patients in our hospital. Our hospital is also involved in the AIDS problem in another way. Kim Brown had been a nurse at our hospital for several years. The problem of AIDS caught her attention so she began working on an AIDS prevention program for the hill tribes of northern Thailand. Now the program is in full operation with trained teams going to villages teaching groups of village leaders how to teach their people about AIDS and its prevention.

This week three end-stage AIDS admissions arrived at our little hospital. Pray for Kim's project. Pray for our staff as we seek to give compassionate care to the suffering. Pray for our Christians that we will be examples of disciplined morality in a pagan and sensuous world.

Perhaps AIDS is God's megaphone calling us to turn from our sinful ways.

Sincerely,
J. Freeman

23 May 1993

Dear Friends,

The readjustment to being a jungle doctor again hasn't been a very easy task. Of course Thai is the basic language here in Thailand and relearning that is hard enough. Then in this area there is Northern Thai, Thai Yai, and in our hospital most of the patients are Karen with their two dialects which even changes a bit from village to village. The distance from village to village is so great that even the customs and dress vary. So in addition to the new diseases, drugs, and language problems, there is the constant learning of the cultural practices which contribute to the disease patterns.

NawWa's parents carried her four hours from their village to a village with a road, then waited for a car to the main road. When I finished examining the little one-year-old pathological package, I sighed to myself. Here was pneumonia, diarrhea caused by giardia, intestinal roundworms, staphylococcal infection of one leg, corneal ulcers of both eyes caused by vitamin A deficiency and malnutrition. It was a struggle to get an adequate history of the illness because no one was on duty who could speak their dialect.

After we had initiated treatment, I began to think about the young parents' decision to bring the baby to our hospital. They live in a village that is so primitive it is hard to imagine unless one has visited there. For these people to go to another city where they have never been and where they have neither family nor friends must have taken great courage. On top of that they had very little money and had no idea how long before the child would be well. Again they had no assurance the daughter would even get well. What love they must have had for their little one!

We never know how long we have to treat a patient like this as the family may decide to go home at any time, regardless of the progress. We took extra time to explain in detail the procedures and the treatment thus trying to gain their confidence. They seemed to appreciate the explanations.

It took three days before it occurred to me that the underlying cause of the corneal ulcers was vitamin A deficiency. This was a condition that I had read about but never seen. I felt bad because unless treated quickly with large doses of vitamin A the condition could lead to blindness.

In our hospital we are trying to make health education teachers out of all our staff. In this way the patient and family will go home with more than just healing for a specific illness. One day we were discussing birth control with the family (through an interpreter, of course). The father replied that they were already using a method which he proceeded to explain. There is a certain tree near their village which has powers to prevent conception. The wife then began fumbling with the bundle of beads around her neck. Finally there was separated a two-inch long piece of wood held around her neck with a string.

A couple more days passed and the leg was well; the worms and giardia were gone. NawWa looked much better, but there was still something not right. The cry was strange and she didn't move as much as should to be normal. I thought it may be due to blindness. But the next day I was more convinced of another factor. Both Dr. Sureerat and I thought she had a stiff neck. The mother had been coughing for over a year. Was this TB meningitis? Just as I was about to tell the mother and father of the need to do a spinal tap to test for meningitis, the nurse aid completed a conversation with them and announced that they had decided to go home that day.

This was no surprise. I sat down on the edge of the bed disappointed in myself for failing first to recognize the Vitamin A deficiency and then for failing to pick up earlier on the signs of meningitis. The family wanted to go home to make sacrifices to appease the village spirits. The particular sacrifice they had in mind was to prepare a large meal for the paternal grandfather. The young father would have to borrow money to buy the chickens and the pig required for the feast. Of course, the other villagers would be invited to the feast. I suspect that one of the factors in the persistence of these spirit feasts is the desire to feast at someone else's expense.

As we talked, it turned out that the father was willing to leave the baby for further treatment but not the mother. If the infant died before getting back to the village the child would then not be allowed to enter the village for the funeral. The mother could not accept the fate of an improper funeral.

Having failed to convince the family to continue the treatment, the thought came to me that if the infant was blind and if she did have TB meningitis she would have a rather dismal future in such a primitive village where survival is difficult even with perfect faculties. Perhaps the instincts of the parents were right after all.

We are working now to improve our village health program and to increase the villages we visit. Pray with us that we may be able to prevent tragedies like NawWa.

Your friend in Christ,
John & Nancy Freeman

30 June 1993

Dear Friends,

Twenty-seven Maesariang monsoons, are not so bad, but twenty-seven Maesariang hot seasons, well, that is enough to give anyone a stroke. Believe me, I have seen only one and I thought I would surely die before it was over. Bina Sawyer was looking forward to her twenty-seventh hot season here when she did have a stroke. I was to relieve her in April of this year but came early because of her illness. Bina is in her seventieth year and was the age of mandatory retirement.

This is a special week here since it is Dr. Bina's last at the hospital where she has so faithfully and diligently served so many years. After recuperation in the USA from the stroke she came back here to close up her house and visit many of the friends she had made. Nancy was commenting on how cheerfully Bina had accepted her illness (still a bit of right-sided weakness). According to Bina the wheelchairs at the airports were really nice. I replied that if I had been up as many times during the nights as she has I would be glad to accept a wheelchair even if I had no illness.

Dr. Bina's leaving is special in another sense. She is the last of the "Old Burma Hands." After her training she was assigned to work in Burma with the American Baptists. After only a few years there, however, a military coup turned the country toward the "Burmese road to Socialism." Missionaries were soon ordered to leave. With the many Karens and other hilltribes also in Thailand, some of the missionaries came to serve here, and Dr. Bina was one of them. With her leaving an era comes to a close.

Trained as a pediatrician, naturally Dr. Bina's main interest was children. However, general medicine was required since the hospital originally was the only hospital in the area. Early on she encouraged the development of a village health program which has continued till this day and has been instrumental in preserving the health of thousands of children as well as adults.

The catalogue of the diseases that Dr. Bina has been familiar with would sound strange to our American doctor colleagues: Potts disease, Marasmus, scrofula, cerebral Malaria, Kwashiorkor, Japanese B encephalitis, amoebic dysentery, Weils disease, typhoid, etc. The people of this area have been fortunate to have had a friend who was willing to wrestle with those strange diseases. From the ones I have talked with, they are thankful for this dedicated servant of God and what she has done for the people here.

THANK YOU DR. BINA. WE WILL MISS YOU.

Sincerely,

John & Nancy Freeman

Maesariang
17 July, 1993

Dear Friends,

This is a lazy Saturday afternoon and it would be nice to take a good nap, but I had an interesting trip to a Karen refugee village this week and would like to tell you about it.

The greedy power-hungry dictators in Rangoon continue to harass the Karens, so many of them are forced to live on the Thai side of the border for the safety of their families. We had been to Kateeta before and discovered that this village of over 2,000 people did not have an immunization program. Since they are all Burmese they are not entitled to Thai medical programs. Refugee committee funds have not been adequate for such a program.

We decided to begin by immunizing children under five years of age with Diphtheria-tetanus-whooping cough and polio and to give Tetanus immunizations to pregnant women to prevent neonatal tetanus. Dr. Tamlasay, who is in charge of their little hospital, sent us a list of those in that category so we took the vaccine this week for the first round of vaccinations.

Our improved mountain road finally ended in a little stream. We followed the stream, at times driving down the middle of it, for a couple of kilometers until we arrived at Mae Sam Lap. There we were met by Dr. Tamlasay and the boat which took us up river about thirty minutes to Kateeta. The village stretched about a mile or so along the shore of the rain swollen river. All the houses were made of bamboo and roofed with panels made of a type of large jungle tree leaf. Banana trees surrounded most houses, testimony that the village had been there several years.

We were welcomed into the home of Geh Plau, the headman of the village. After a hurried lunch we went to the church where the vaccinations were carried out. A good number turned out for the shots in spite of this being malaria season. We had sent malaria medicine in advance for the children so they would be fever-free for the vaccinations. Our two daughters, Krista (studying nursing) and Jonlyn helped with the clinic. The next day we took our things to the hospital for another vaccination clinic. It was in a different part of the village and closer to the other families. This time we enlisted the nurses of the hospital to help so they could get experience in vaccination. They were glad to learn new skills and we hope to turn over the clinics to them in the future. Dr. Tamlasay and his "nurses" seem to have little skills in public health. We hope that they will catch the spirit of preventive medicine.

That night we were invited to the church for a worship service. Any occasion is an occasion for worship for the Karens. The village's one Coleman gas lantern was hanging in the center of the church. I was a bit surprised to see a fifty-person choir there waiting to sing. The girls had on white homemade Karen pullovers and red skirts. The boys had on red Karen jackets. Then Geh Plau explained to me that this was the student body of the Kateeta Bible Academy. I didn't know that such a thing existed. When it was time to start the service the choir stood up and, without a director or musical instruments, burst out singing one of the most beautiful hymns I have ever heard. It was a Karen hymn and sung in the typical Karen harmony. The faces of these young people were covered with joyous smiles. Along about the third verse my surprise calmed a bit as I looked down at the dirt floor. Then I became aware of the background sound of the monsoon rain softly falling on the leaf roof. Who needs stained glass windows and lofty spires to worship?

The next day after the clinic was over I walked over to the Bible Academy and looked in on a couple of the classes. Lectures were being given in their open air classrooms. One class was spending their time praying-an inspirational sight.

There is also in Kateeta a high school where over 500 students are enrolled. I asked Mrs. Hicks, an Australian volunteer teacher where all the kids came from. "Out of the woodwork I guess," was her reply. Mrs. Hicks, in her sixties, was living there in a bamboo house and going to the river to bathe each day like everyone else. She explained that even though the Karens are completely responsible for running the Bible Academy and the high school, the Australian Baptists give some financial aid to the high school.

It is interesting what God is doing in out of the way places of the world. For this we give thanks.

Your Friend in Christ,

John & Nancy Freeman

Carrying roof leaves.

Stitching leaves onto roof panels.

A rice storage house with leaf roof panels.

18 July 1993

Dear Friends,

"No one said life would be easy in the desert." Walt Devault was always quoting that whenever any problem arose. This was while we were working together in the King Faisal Hospital in Khamis Mushayt in Southwest Saudi Arabia. Coincidentally, we both signed up for a project in Peshawar, Pakistan in 1987 teaching Afghan Mujahadeen medics. Walt brought his saying there as well. Walt was a fun loving guy but stomach cancer took him away soon after our stint in Peshawar was over.

Here in Northwest Thailand on the Thai-Burmese border I have modified his saying to "No one said life would be easy in the jungle." This week that fact was brought home to me again. A fifty year old man was brought in very ill with malaria. He didn't respond to the usual anti-malarial medications and his blood kept testing positive for P. falciparium, the deadly malaria variety. His temperature-pulse pattern was atypical so we decided that he probably had typhoid as well (we are in the midst of a typhoid epidemic here). The addition of antibiotic for typhoid didn't help; then his hemoglobin began to drop. Either malaria or typhoid could account for this problem. Finally it was to the point where a blood transfusion was necessary to save his live. In the age of AIDS we must be very careful as a transfusion can be a death sentence as well as life saving.

When our patient was admitted to the hospital he had with him a host of relatives including several sons. When I announced that we needed blood no one was to be found. Needless to say, blood is hard to come by here. It seems that everyone has "bad blood" for some reason or other. Finally, in desperation I told the young grandson who remained with the patient to go tell the sons that their father had not long to live and they must come immediately. Finally a son showed up during out patient clinic. He protested but, determined to get a donor, I took him by the hand to lead him to the lab for blood typing. He had a fever! Sure enough it was 103F. Then his malaria smear revealed malaria parasites. So rather than a donor I had another patient. Later another brother showed up. He had group A blood and his father was B.

Reluctantly, we took a unit of blood from one of our staff and gave to the patient. A couple of weeks ago when we couldn't find blood for a patient about to die I threatened to leave the hospital (quit that is) if a system of getting blood for needy patients wasn't instituted immediately. I reminded them that Jesus donated his blood so that we may have eternal life and forgiveness from sin and we should be willing to do the same for others. Several of our staff volunteered but unfortunately most of our staff are positive for the hepatitis B virus.

The next day more sons came to donate. Another was group A. The one they all said was the best to give blood turned out to have HIV positive blood. Another staff member then offered his blood. "No one said life in the jungle would be easy."

After my "threaten to quit-blood talk" one of the staff members stopped me and said, "Yes that was right about the blood of Jesus but he was God and we are not. Moreover the one needing blood was a drug addict and no good so we should save our blood for the good patients."

When you have a spare minute pray for us.

Sincerely,
John & Nancy Freeman

Note: The patient died in the hospital after testing positive for HIV.

Christian Hospital
Maesariang
30 August 1993

Dear Friends,

 Death. Yes, death and dying eventually come, and then the funeral. A while back we were invited to the funeral of one of our patients who succumbed to cancer. I had gotten to know the family during the long illness so decided to go to the Sunday afternoon affair.

 We arrived too late for the ceremonial feast so we went straight to the cremating field. We got out of the car and stood in the sun with the other family members, neighbors and others interested in the events. We were immediately served an iced drink by some of the family members. Soon a wagon brightly decorated with the casket was pulled by several men into the field immediately in front of us. Flowers were arranged on the wagon in front of it, then a group of Buddhist monks in a sala began their chants in their typical nasal monotone. Not understanding a word of the Sanskrit chants, I rapidly tired of it in the hot sun. But soon it was over and a monk moved up to the wagon and casket. They chanted again as threads were passed over the casket.

 After the religious ceremonies were completed, large photos of the deceased were placed in front of the casket and photos were taken. There were family photos, then groups of friends and those with whom the deceased had worked. Suddenly I found myself and the nurses posing. In a few minutes the pullers reappeared and towed the wagon across the field about 75 yards to the cremating platform. The casket was then placed on a pile of wood while a couple of men were arranging some decorations over the casket. After the wagon had been replaced in front of us I began to wonder who would light the fire.

 A noise attracted my attention from the sala where the monks were seated. As I turned to look, a rocket burst into action and, with a screaming sound, raced along a wire to a post on our left. I had hardly recovered from the first blast when the second occurred and another rocket ignited and raced along a wire to the next post. This happened several times until the rocket reached a series of upright steel posts. Fire and smoke erupted from each post in turn. I thought at one time there must be a post for every year of age. Another display took place near the casket; then the communication was broken. A technician raced out to restart the show and the fire reached the casket. Suddenly a giant sparkler display broke out and a shower of sparks rained down on the funeral pyre. A flammable liquid had obviously been doused on the dead and the wood as it immediately leapt into flames.

Quite a show, I thought to myself. Then I began to calculate the cost of such a display, plus the large feast that fed everyone in the neighborhood and anyone else who wanted to attend. Invitations had to be printed, the monks had to have an offering, and photos to be paid for. Death is certainly not cheap here.

A few weeks ago the young daughter of one of our nurse-aids was tragically killed on a motorbike. As soon as we found out about this Nancy and I visited the church where the body was on display. Already arrangements were being made to prepare food to feed everyone. The police delayed the funeral a couple of days until the investigation was complete. That meant that the family had to continually feed everyone until the funeral. Then at the funeral the family was expected to serve drinks to all those attending the burial. What an exhausting process.

Just this past week the business manager of the hospital had his father-in-law to die. He quickly borrowed a very large sum of money and went off to the other city for the funeral. Nancy remarked that this appeared more related to paganism than to Christianity when those suffering are made to suffer even more as a result of their misfortunes.

Some of the villages in our area are still devoted to animism. In these villages, when a person suffers a misfortune, he must sacrifice some of his animals to appease the spirits. The more serious the misfortune the larger the sacrifice is required. If he does not have the required sacrifice, then he is expected to borrow money in order to buy the animals. The sufferer is thus penalized for having been unfortunate.

A couple of days ago we were discussing the Christian funerals here with a Christian friend. We told them that it seemed to us that their practice came straight from their animist backgrounds. Well, they didn't see it quite that way so we left it at that. I am thankful that when my father and mother died a few years ago, our neighbors came to help rather than to sponge off us. Our Christian heritage has given us many good things. Jesus taught us to bear one another's burdens. In our little Christian Hospital we have opportunity daily to bear others' burdens. Remember to pray for us.

In Christ.
John & Nancy Freeman

Christian Hospital
Maesariang
5 September 1993

Dear friends,

    A couple of weeks ago we were in Chiang Mai for business. In a strange place I usually wake early, so I made my way out on the street to find a sidewalk coffee shop. A few blocks down the road I found a shop in a market area. Close by was a man selling Thai style donuts hot out of the frying pan. A Thai market is always an interesting place to sit and watch as all kinds of interesting things are happening. Coffee, donuts, pineapples, and sticky rice: all purchases from different vendors made up my breakfast. As I was eating, I heard a man across the street selling something. It wasn't clear exactly what he was selling, so I leaned across the little table and asked an elderly Thai man, also having his morning coffee, what the man was selling. He was not in much of a mood for conversation, so he answered with two words, "Kai wang"(Selling hope). I thought about that for a few minutes, then became absorbed in watching the people and activities of the market.

    Hope is a precious commodity in any culture. We have had a few patients who had lost all hope, such as one of our drug addicts, and when this happens, it is a sad sight. Though Thailand has a very well organized religion, an abundance of people are selling "hope" through various other means. Most of the men who come to the hospital have tattoos of symbols or of animals which are needled into their skin to prevent evil. It is not uncommon to have a patient with a number of amulets tied around his neck. All were sold or given to him in order either to prevent something or to gain something. Almost every house and business in Thailand has a little spirit house somewhere in the corner of the yard where offerings are offered regularly to appease the spirits. Special offerings may be given at times to ensure the success of a new venture.

    This country has a wide variety of practitioners selling hope and healing. The "oil massage Doctor" takes care of broken bones and muscular aches and pains. I once saw a patient with an intricately woven forearm splint made of bamboo. It kept his fracture in perfect alignment and was infinitely more comfortable in this tropical climate than a plaster cast would have been. Herbal doctors deal with fevers and winds ("lom" or wind is responsible for an awful lot of misery). Exorcists are not as common as in previous days, but still there are many angry spirits which keep the practitioners busy. "Shot Doctors" are a newer arrival to the scene. They will usually give a shot of whatever the patient requests. A bottle of IV saline is popular in order to cure "weakness."

In the old days the Buddhist priests took care of most of the healing because they had time to study the subject. Although modern medicine has taken most of the healing out of their domain, many of the Buddhists stop by the temple before going to the hospital in order for the priest to tie strings around the wrists and ankles. This, as I understand, is to prevent the wind (or spirit) from escaping from their body prematurely. This is just an example of a few of those involved in the hope and healing ministry here. If you went to a good sized temple fair, you could find a jillion others.

When breakfast was over, I walked across the street to get a better look at the "hope vendor." If what he was selling really worked according to his promise, it would well be worth the fifty baht (two dollars) he was charging. It would bring happiness to the home and ensure a winning lottery ticket. He was quite an artist at his trade. I thought to myself that he might make more money as a politician.

There was a five-by-eight foot grass mat in the center of his circle. I noticed that it was a little lumpy; then I realized that a four inch wide snake head was peeping out from under the mat. So this was an old-fashioned snake doctor. Near the end of his pitch he laid a young lad on a mat and performed some tricks to demonstrate that his amulet worked. He got the lad up and washed "blood" off his back to prove he was unharmed. Then the snakes were uncovered. The seven foot long python went peacefully into his box. Then the other snakes were put away. I noticed that none of my old jungle friends-banded krait, cobras, nor Russel's viper-were in his collection.

The show was over and "hope" had been sold to several dozen people. What kind of hope were they looking for? Hope for the success of their children. Hope for success in business. Hope for health and protection from AIDS when the husband is unfaithful. Much the same as in any country, I suppose. I'm glad for the hope that Jesus gave us. Hope that is forgiveness, reconciliation, love, and justice. We must have hope; therefore we must have the giver of hope.

Sincerely
John Freeman

18 September 1993

Dear Friends,

Leprosy is one of the diseases that appears to have almost disappeared from the scene. I have seen only one person with that once dreaded disease, since we have returned to Thailand, and he was far out in a village. I was reminded of leprosy with a visit the other day to what used to be called the McKean Leprosy Hospital in Chiang Mai. Driving through that leprosarium was like taking a trip backward in history. The place was built back in the days when a local prince still ruled Chiang Mai. He donated the land to the missionaries for the hospital. The buildings are of brick and plaster, the architecture resembling something in rural India.

One section of the place contains a "leper colony" which consists of rows of neat small cottages where the "lepers" would live while being treated. Many finished out their lives on earth in this place since there was nowhere else to go. They would work as they could in the large gardens, orchards, and shops. This little colony is still occupied with older folks, many of whom have the physical scars of leprosy. Of course, with modern medicine their disease (akin to TB) has been cured.

When we first came to Thailand (1970) we worked in the Bangkla Baptist Hospital east of Bangkok. One of our special ministries there was our leprosy work, many patients came regularly to our hospital for treatment. There was also a program for doing reconstructive surgery for those with paralyzed or deformed limbs. Grace, an Australian doctor, would come now and then to perform this specialized surgery. "Amazing Grace," as she was known, was an itinerant leprosy specialist skilled in tendon transplantation.

We had a branch "Skin Clinic" in Chonburi which was to take care of our patients in that city and to screen for new patients. If I remember right I was down there when our youngest, Jonlyn, came into the world.

One of the highlights of my work with the lepers was a village clinic trip to a remote village composed mostly of leper families. Once the clinic was completed the villagers all gathered in a large, crudely made house for a worship service, it being a Sunday. All

Clinic in leper village. Dr. Somporn in flowered blouse, a staff member of Bangla Baptist Hospital.

Deformed leper hands holding a Bible.

of the buildings in the obviously poor village were crudely made as hands are the first to suffer deformities from leprosy. As the villagers filled the room, a few collected in the front with crudely made musical instruments. There was not a store-bought instrument among the lot. A five-gallon oil can was used as a drum. I couldn't get my eyes off that motley collection of instruments and the stubby deformed hands, some paralyzed, that caused music to issue forth. That combination of music and hymn singing was the most soul-stirring I have ever heard.

One of our patients in Bangkla was a rather prosperous road contractor. His room was always filled with highway diagrams and progress charts of his latest job. He had to be hospitalized now and then because of reactions to treatment medicines. Later, after we had moved to Sangklaburi, I had occasion to visit him seeking consultation about a bridge project I was involved in. While conversing with him I noticed a small child coming and going. Since he was a little past middle age I inquired if that was his child. "Oh no," he replied. "We just took her to raise. You know, no home is complete without a child and an old person."

Such a concept is one thing that makes the Thai society so attractive and such a contrast to that in our own country where people are determined to live alone, the basis for a host of medical problems. One of the first things that God said in the book of Genesis was that it is not good that man live alone.

In the past, thousands were forced to leave their families and communities because of the fear and ignorance that surrounded leprosy. Thankfully, that is a thing of the past. Today though, we have a scourge, AIDS, that isolates people in much the same way. Pray for the weak church here in Thailand that our members will accept the calling of Christ to minister to the sick and suffering regardless of the stigma of their disease.

Yours in Christ,
John & Nancy Freeman

22 September 1993

Dear Friends,

Thailand without elephants would be a dull place, and it is getting that way. I haven't seen an elephant in Maesariang since we arrived. The only place they are, it seems, is out on the Salween River where they pull logs down to the river.

While we were up on the Kwai River there were still wild herds of elephants. I encountered a group of hunters who came up to try to capture one of the beasts; unfortunately, the only thing one of them captured was a good case of cerebral malaria. We were able to treat him successfully in our little hospital, and that is how I heard about the wild elephants. Actually, they gave up without seeing any and returned to Bangkok with their recuperating friend.

Our house there was only about thirty feet from a path along which elephants passed almost daily. For being such large animals, they walk silently and gracefully. We would never know that they were passing unless we heard the logging chains jangling. The kids would then run to the window to watch. They never tired of watching their graceful strides. About a hundred yards down from our house the path crossed the Rantee River (one of three small rivers that came together there to form the Kwai River) where our children spent most of the hot season playing in the water. Elephants would frequently pause there also to take a bath and soak themselves in water, needing a daily soaking.

One day in the hospital Jan, our Australian nurse, told me that I had another patient waiting. When I walked around to the OPD and didn't see anyone, I asked where the patient was. I was told to look outside. There was the largest elephant I had ever seen standing just in front of the door. His eyes were even with the eve of the roof. The elephant driver said that there was an itching rash on his chest. I took a look at the rash and then did some calculations. It would take all of the salves and ointments in our stock to cover the area one time. We always tried to accommodate the local people in treating their animals but that was one itch I couldn't scratch.

Another time a local timberman's wife came rushing into the hos-

Elephant and driver with chains for logging.

pital requesting that I go to a village to collect one of their employees who had been mauled by an elephant. We weren't too busy, our old jungle truck was running, and it was the dry season so I agreed if she would go along and give directions. Soon we were off with some first aid supplies and a litter. After about an hour's drive, fortunately on rather smooth jungle logging trails, we came to the village. We were immediately ushered over to a bamboo house where the victim lay on the floor.

My first glance at the semi-comatose, bruised and battered man told me that he was seriously injured. I knelt down and started going over him from top to bottom. There was hardly any place that was not swollen and deformed. A few things were easy to diagnose: a broken mandible, numerous rib fractures, probably a lumbar fracture. Internal injuries I was not sure of but if so the rough ride over the jungle trail wouldn't do them any good. An IV was started; then he was loaded into the truck for the slow, cautious ride to the hospital. Sure enough almost all his ribs were broken; there was a lumbar fracture of the spine and the mandible was broken. He looked as though the elephant had picked him up with his trunk and whipped him against a tree. Jungle people tend to be tough, though, and this patient was no exception. He recovered completely. Later on a visit to his village I saw him with a little kink in his back.

A few months after that incident Olivia (our Midwife/public health worker) asked me one day if I remembered the elephant patient. Olivia knew everything about everyone in the area as well as all the animals. One day while walking to Three Pagoda Pass village Olivia suddenly and urgently pushed us off the trail and behind a large stand of bamboo. After we were safely hidden she explained that she had sighted an elephant that she knew coming down the trail. I hadn't seen it but she had. Only Olivia could have recognized it from that far away. She went on to say that it had killed one of its drivers, murdered two police motorcycles and slain another elephant in a battle. After hearing the elephant's history I took great care to stay concealed and very quiet. Finally the beast came into view pulling a large cart loaded with cargo. The driver was astride the neck with a large machete in one hand. The tusks had been cut off to keep him from doing more harm than necessary. I thought the red stains on the forehead of the elephant were betel nut stains from the driver spitting but Olivia corrected me. Those blood stains coming from the whacks on the head by the driver to keep him "in line."

Well, back to Olivia's question. When I told her that I still remembered the case, she informed me that the same elephant had disemboweled its driver and was on a rampage down river from the hospital. For a month or two the animal was loose destroying rice fields and even chasing boats that came up and down the river. People in the area were terrified of the beast.

One day our hospital maintenance man (he had eight small children) told me that he was considering trying to capture the elephant. Naturally I inquired as to how he intended the capture. He explained that he would make a wooden bullet (now he was an old elephant driver himself) for his gun, then hide in the bushes. When the elephant came by he would shoot the elephant between his front toes. The wooden bullet would start festering, thus temporarily crippling him. He then asked me what I thought of his plan. I pictured myself hiding in the tall grass shooting an elephant of that nature in the foot and then with me having eight mouths to feed. When I didn't think much of the idea, I noticed that he stayed at his duties the next few weeks

A few days later at lunch I noticed a large elephant parked in front of the maintenance man's house with his trunk draped over the porch rail. Jonlyn, then about two years and Krista about four years old, were playing on the porch with several of the other children. Elephants being common in the neighborhood, I didn't think much about it. On return to the hospital Olivia asked me if I had seen that rogue elephant. I rushed to the door of the hospital and looked over at the house but the beast had gone. I breathed a sigh of relief for Jonlyn and Krista had been looking eyeball to eyeball with that thing.

Next I wanted to know how the animal was captured. The maintenance man had a nephew who was also an elephant driver. He made some kind of deal with the owner to share the services of the elephant when captured. He then tracked the beast for a few days to determine its habits. According to the story, he perched himself in a tree overhanging the elephant's trail to the river; then when the elephant walked under the tree he dropped down on the neck and with one hard blow of his large machete the rogue was tame again. Now, that was a

Elephants had the right-of-way on our trails.

Elephant passing school in Sangkaburi.

few years ago and there may be more to that story by now. Some of us deserve a whack on the head or a bullet between the toes to point us in the right direction, but such is not God's preferred method. The old Testament mentions that He guides us with His eye and in another place it speaks of His still small voice. Jesus promised that He would send us His Spirit that would dwell within us to guide us in His path.

In Christ,
John D. Freeman

   * Berserk Elephant Killed read the headline in the Bangkok Post 7 Feb. l994. "Thai police near the Burmese border were forced to use assault rifles to kill a berserk elephant, police said yesterday.
   Somphon a 30-year old bull elephant, was shot to death on Saturday because police were worried it would harm villagers.
   They said Somphon went berserk on Friday and damaged three cars in Thong Pha Phum district of Kanchanaburi Province, near the Burmese border."
(Tong Pha Phum is just a few miles south of Sangklaburi)

2 October 1993

Dear Friends,

Thailand is a happy place. At least it is this Saturday afternoon sitting here between calls from the hospital as I listen to the happy play-talk from the hundred or so hostel kids next door. Some people call this the land of smiles because of the make up of the Thai face which produces a ready smile at the least provocation. I have found that a smile can be obtained in almost any situation just by looking at a Thai or group of them, regardless of the activities they may be engaged in. Such an atmosphere makes the land a pleasant place to live in.

There is unfortunately a lot of misery covered up by those ready smiles. Working as we do in the hospital, it falls our lot to lift up the covers and see what is brewing underneath. Take for instance Lek (not her real name), an attractive smallish girl of about twenty, smartly dressed and with a ready smile. Art and Jeannie, missionary friends of ours, had told me of her before she came to the clinic. She had been sent to their Bible School from missionaries in Bangkok. After arrival and enrollment in the school it turned out that Lek had AIDS and was already showing some symptoms. So it was that I met this what looked to me like a "little girl" that day in the clinic. After the exam I discussed with her what to do with the rash that she had. Then what else do you say to someone who is under the death sentence (medications for HIV treatment was not available at that time)? That is something that I am still learning, and frankly rather uncertain as to how to deal with.

A couple of weeks later Nancy and I decided to attend Art and Jeannie's church as we had a telephone message to give them. After the service was about over, opportunity was given for anyone to give a short message if they so desired. To my surprise Lek was the second to march up to the front of the worshippers to speak. This time she didn't look so "girlish" but had a look of mature determination on her face. Lek began to disclose how she had come to her present situation.

Lek's parents had separated when she was a small girl. She and two other siblings had been left to be raised by the father. That was somewhere in the Shan State in Burma. According to her story, that was a rather peaceful life until she arrived at the age of fourteen. At that time a couple of men in the neighborhood, along with the conniving of her own mother, decided that Lek could be sold for a good sum of money. So she was kidnapped from her father's house; when the buying and selling process was over, Lek was in a Bangkok brothel.

Some of the brothels are literal prisons where the victims are subjected to continual rape, others are places where the girls remain freely after their soul has been destroyed and there is no where else to go. After six years Lek's only possessions were the clothes on her back and the AIDS virus. Then one day there was a police raid on her brothel, and she was taken to a detention center to await "processing."

"Processing" means that the girls may, if they can raise money, be let go free. Many times, though, what happens is that the brothel owner comes and pays his dues and the girls are then returned to the brothel. The only thing having changed is the police have been enriched in the process. During Lek's detention a Thai preacher came to the center to preach. Lek had in her youth in Burma seen the Jesus Film and had been impressed by it. After hearing the preacher, she talked with him and indicated that she was interested and wanted to quit the life she was enslaved to.

My poor comprehension of Thai didn't allow me to understand all of what transpired but sufficient to say she turned her life over to Christ and then was entrusted to some missionaries in Bangkok who deal with wounded souls like Lek. As to how she got here I am not sure, but suspect that when it was discovered that she had the AIDS virus, it was decided that the best place for her was a Bible School out in the jungle. And I think they were right.

Well, Lek labored at her presentation in the church for quite a while, long enough that most people got tired. Even I decided at one time to leave, but Nancy restrained me as that would not be polite. She was determined to tell her story and it was easy to see that she was a troubled person. Several times during her presentation she referred to her feeling of being unclean. Oh what evil people are in the world that would for a little pleasure and profit wreak havoc on such a helpless little girl! Bravely she told her story and concluded with telling of her desire to return to her village and tell her people about the love of Christ.

A week or so later Nancy and I went out to visit Art and Jeannie. Lek happened by and wanted to ask a question about her medicine. She then told me that I had reminded her so much of her father only he was much smaller. She had seen me in church that morning and said that seeing me gave her strength to continue her story. Naturally I felt ashamed of myself for thinking about leaving that service.

Later I got to thinking about Lek. Giving someone inspiration simply because I happen to look like her father seems like such a small matter, but to her it seemed to mean so much. We often go out in search of the great things to do, but I have been thinking lately that more than likely when all is over and we know the real facts it will be that it is the little things in life that made the most difference. Jesus had several stories to illustrate this.

Pray for Lek as she studies. Pray that she may tell her story of Jesus to her village some day before.....

Sincerely,
J. Freeman

Lek means "little" in Thai and is a popular girls nickname.

9 October 1993

Dear Friends,

Snakes like to live in jungles, and since we are surrounded by jungle a snakebite comes in now and then. A while back a young man came in with a burnt-tail-green-snake bite of several days' duration. Anti-venom for him was of no use, so we put him to bed with his foot propped up and gave him what medicine we thought best. In spite of our efforts, he developed a lot of fluid under the skin which we drained with several long incisions. Some muscle and tendons dissolved, but he finally got up and rode off on his motorcycle.

When we first came to Thailand, Andrew and Lloyd were little fellers who liked to explore everywhere possible. One day they came running into the house and told Nancy that they had seen a big snake. "What kind was it?" Nancy asked. They didn't know but it was standing up and had a big fat neck. Now Nancy likes almost all kinds of animals, but a chill went up her spine that time. In all the places I have worked here in Thailand I have never seen a patient with a cobra bite. I guess it is such a deadly thing that they don't make it to the hospital.

When we lived up on the Kwai there were several different kinds of snakes that hung around our neighborhood. One night I was called out to embalm a man (not one of my patients, by the way). That was a little business I had on the side and was one of my reasons for making house calls. I never had any training in that sort of thing but had developed a little routine (a trade secret) in response to repeated requests from the villagers.

Anyway, having completed my chore and declined the offer of a meal, which was in progress in the same room as the corpse, I made my way back home. A dim flashlight guided me along the dark dirt path. Just in front of the headman's house something moved in the path. I froze and watched as a beautiful banded krait sluggishly made his way across the path. It was about seven feet long and the largest snake I have seen in the wild over here. He was headed for the headman's house, but since I had nothing to change his direction with just let him go. Those things are very deadly, so I was a little more careful the rest of the way home. A few days later I mentioned my sight-ing to a friend and also commented that I had never seen a banded krait-bitten patient. His response was that they only bite rich people and government workers.

One would think that we would see more snake bites out here in the jungle, but actually there are not so many. One of their beliefs is that a person with a snakebite must not cross a river or stream or he will die. In Thailand it is almost impossible to get from one place to another without crossing a stream or canal of some kind, so perhaps that helps to explain why we see so few.

We had just completed rounds one morning in our little hospital on the Kwai when two men came hauling in a patient slung on a bamboo pole. After he was stretched out on the floor in the middle of the waiting room floor I got a good look at the young man of about twenty. He was moribund with blood oozing from his pores and old scars. The man in charge of the patient's transport to the hospital then mentioned "took gnu kat" (snakebite). The two common snakes with hemotoxic venom are Russel's viper and the Malayan pit viper, so I knew what the situation was.

As I knelt beside the young man I thought to myself that I would not give a tical (equivalent to a nickel) for his life. Then I got up and looked at the man who had brought him and told him that I would not accept him unless he gave a unit of blood then and there. He was not kin to the patient and when he agreed I was shocked, but I didn't let on. Of course I was bluffing but in the jungle one has to get blood anyway possible. We once took blood from another patient who was having a chill (malaria) to give to another worse off than he was. Both were given malaria medicine and left the hospital a few days later in good spirits.

We worked with the poor fellow for two weeks giving blood and trying to stop the blood from leaking out. He was loaded with antivenom and in all took in about eight pints of blood. I had a bright idea once of giving some vitamin K thinking that may help his clotting mechanism. He bled about two pints of blood into his thigh, the injection site. So I discovered that was not a good idea. Finally, one day he decided to live. Perhaps he opened his eyes and saw one of our pretty nurses. At that time his hemoglobin level was about 5 grams (normal about 14) and we were out of sources for blood, so he gradually recovered. When he was able to walk he went out and helped in our hospital vegetable garden where he worked off his bill. After a couple of months he bade us good-bye and disappeared into the jungle.

Jesus told his disciples that they should be wise as serpents and harmless as doves. I'm not sure how wisdom became equated with snakes, but in the situation I am in now I surely do need wisdom; the snakes you can leave. There are always staff problems, problems with myself and then daily there are patients with mystery diseases. Pray for us here and give thanks that God provides for all our needs.

In Christ's Love,
John & Nancy Freeman

16 October 1993

Dear friends,

Last month the supporting mission organizations got together and cut off the water to the little hospital here. From what we have found since we arrived here in January, I cannot say that I blame them. Dr. Keith Dahlberg, the father of the hospital, said that it was started with a life span of twenty years planned for it; the twenty was up about ten years ago. One of my maxims is that you cannot keep a hospital going, or any other business for that matter, unless there is quality and efficiency in the system two things that when we arrived, we found in need of attention. I set out to rectify the situation, but, to be honest, my efforts have been mostly failures.

When we were up on the Kwai River, I set out from the reopening of the hospital with the goal in mind to make it as self-sufficient as possible, and that was in a very poor area. All the time we were there, Communist rebels were just up the trail. They never bothered us, but there was a pessimistic mood in Southeast Asia, and we had no idea how long missionaries would be there. We told the people that if they wanted a hospital and good medical care, they would have to pay for it. If they didn't have money, then they could give rice, pumpkins, coconuts, or whatever. For the most part, they did.

We had been out to Beke village once for a clinic. Unbeknown to us, our boat driver had happened upon some friends who had homemade brew that needed to be disposed of. He obliged them, of course. We loaded our boat with our supplies and payments for the return trip home. The driver, being under the influence, grossly miscalculated the width of the swift little river and rammed us into some bushes on the opposite bank. Before I knew what was happening, the stern, crossways to the rapid current, was going down with the motor. I grabbed for our floating medicine bags, then looked around. There in front of me was Olivia, our public health worker, perched on a branch with part of our payment (six chickens) perched around her. She had salvaged as many other payments as possible, and they too were decorating the bushes. We had to paddle back home because the motor had drowned. However, we didn't always have this much trouble returning with our payments.

One of the things that helped us greatly in those days was the uncanny memory of our Karen nurse, Ebra. More than once a patient would come into the hospital saying that he had never been there before. Ebra and sometimes Olivia would say to me, "I think I have seen that person before." Then later they would come in with a chart and say, "Yes, he was here five years ago under another name, and he owes such and such." Those two women were worth their weight in gold.

We have Karens here too, of course, but not like Ebra and Olivia. The other day Nancy was working in the pharmacy when she was aware of a sudden stillness. She stopped her pill counting and looking up to see what was wrong. In the adjoining room where payments are taken, a young man was threatening to kill our cashier. He thought the bill was far too high. Nancy was the only one to get her bones activated, so she quickly went over and asked to see the bill. The three-hundred bhat bill was one-hundred too high. Now, that is not the way to make a hospital self-sufficient. It turned out that Weporn, the cashier, was just pulling figures out of the air to calculate the bills. We found that she didn't even know the price of quinine, one of the most prescribed drugs in our hospital. Well, as I was saying about quality...

Once up on the Kwai I almost got myself into trouble by being a bit overzealous in regards to collections. Three villagers brought in their elderly father, who was at the point of death, and wanted me to look at him. After looking over the situation, I told the three sons that there was little hope. They discussed the matter among themselves a few minutes, then asked me to do what I could. He died that night, and the next morning they came for the body. The sons didn't want to pay the bill since we hadn't cured him. I explained that I hadn't promised anything and insisted that they pay the bill. Moreover I told them that the body would remain in the hospital until the bill was paid. They went off and didn't come back that day. Of course, the nurses didn't like the idea of a dead body lying around. I stayed awake all night wondering what I had gotten myself into. All kinds of thoughts ran through my mind. Needless to say, I was greatly relieved when the three came to pay the bill and collect the body. The Thai have a saying, "ket laow" which means, "I have learned my lesson." And so I did.

Modern medicine tends to be expensive, so I try to keep tabs on the cost of our treatment compared to that of other medical practitioners in the area. As I recall, a Spirit Doctor (Maw Pee) up on the Kwai could command a fee of 100 bhat, plus the customary chicken and fifth of homemade whiskey. At that time we could cure a case of malaria at about the same price. Also working in the area were the shot doctors, massage doctors (for bone problems), and then there are always the traveling quack doctors. I tried to keep track of their fees as well.

Jesus went about healing the sick and he told us to do the same. The only difference is that we in this age need money to do the job. Now that our money is being shut off, perhaps it is just as well to let the larger government hospital here take over the job. Our little hospital was the first one in the area and did a great job for the first twenty years of its life. Pray for us as we make this transition.

Sincerely,
John & Nancy Freeman

23 October 1993
Kateeta

Tuesday, October 19, we were off with our village health team which included Prapa and Wepan, two of our Karen nurses; Sriporn, a loud-mouthed but jolly visiting nurse; Prechai, the driver, and myself. We drove an hour through the Maesariang Valley, lush with rice fields, then up over the little range of mountains that separates us from the Salween. We arrived at Mae Sam Lap, a village composed of shops, arranged along a narrow dirt road cut into the embankment. A Buddhist temple, a Karen Baptist church, and a government health clinic fill out the village. The letter to Kateeta announcing the plans for our trip had not arrived, so we had to wait for a boat to be arranged. Prechai and I sat in a dirt floor café and ate fried rice as a nearby truckload of blankets was unloaded for the Karen freedom fighters.

The girls finally returned to tell us that the boat was ready, so off we went down the hill to load the vaccine and other supplies. Since it was the end of the rainy season, the water level was down, but the river still turbulent and muddy. Our little long-tailed boat flew the flag of the Karen Free State, which meant that we had to cross the river to the Karen check point, only a formality, before proceeding up the river. The soldier at the checkpoint looked to be about fourteen and was holding a vintage rifle that was almost as large as he was.

The trip up the river is always soothing to my nerves. I was reminded of the many trips we had to make up the Kwai River when we worked there. The Kwai was a much more scenic river than this one. The recent rainy season has produced a thick green cover for the steep hills on either side of the river. Occasionally, I saw a tall tree which made me think about what a forest this had once been. At one point where a little stream joined the river, teak logs were being pulled down by a single tusker elephant. Noticing the small size of the logs, I thought to myself that they were taking the last of the timber grade teak. This, the single most important source of income for the Karen Free State, will be gone in a couple of years.

As we continued, I thought about the courageous Karens who, for forty years protected their little jungle territory, defying the warlords of Rangoon. Now oil has been discovered in the Adaman sea, and the

Thai want to pipleline the gas across the Karen territory. The Chinese are pouring millions into Burma and want access to the ocean across the Kachin area in northeast Burma. Is the curtain ready to be drawn on this interesting little jungle drama?

Soon we arrived at Kateeta, a village of refugees numbering around 2200 Burmese Karens, now living on the Thai side of the banks of the Salween. Since our letter did not preceed us, there was no preparation for immunization clinic that day, so I took a nap. When I woke, Dr. Tamlasay was sitting there waiting. As he seemed to be free, I suggested that we take a walk to the north end of the village.

We had been interested in getting a health program going in this village for some time, one that involved financial responsibility on the part of the villagers. I wanted to get a closer look at the village to see if there are any indicators of ability to support such a simple program. Now, what I am talking about is around 5 baht (twenty cents) a month for immunizations and other health care. Last month I had talked to the headman, Gae Plau, about this, and he told me that these people were refugees and had no money nor any way to make money. No, they didn't have rice fields because the Thai wouldn't give permission for refugees to farm the Thai side, and the Burmese would burn up the fields on the Burmese side. No, they didn't make baskets, no, they didn't weave cloth, and so on.

We stopped at one house to chat, and I noticed a child holding one of our hospital immunization charts. I asked to see it, and the information on the chart indicated two trips to the hospital to get immunizations. A quick calculation of boat fare, car fare, and hospital fees told me that this family had disposable income. We walked on and stopped to talk with another friend of Dr. Tamlasay's. He was moaning about the fact that elephants had gotten into his rice fields and eaten up all the rice. My ears perked up. I said, "And I suppose he destroyed the fields of several others as well?" "Yes," was his reply. I said, "I suppose most of the villagers have rice fields over there?" Again the answer was affirmative. A relief organization provides these people with their rice rations and a few other things. I asked the doctor to show me the village store. Earlier I had walked past it unknowingly. It looked no different from the other village houses. In addition to being rather well-stocked, it had a good supply of medicines, probably more than in Dr. Tamlasay's little hospital.

The children that I saw in the village were running about and playing, well-fed and happy for the most part. One exception was a lap baby, pale and a bit thin, who suffered from chronic malaria. Dr. Tamlasay said that in the past month one child had died in the village from malaria. He was brought to the hospital in moribund state and died within the hour. His little hospital had the means to treat him if he had been brought sooner. Dr. Tamlasay went on to complain that the villagers were often too stubborn to bring their sick to him until it was too late. Respiratory infections and intestinal parasites, including ameobas, are common.

Malaria is the most serious and most common problem in the village. I was happy to see that Dr. Tamlasay's hospital was now doing malaria blood tests, using the microscope that we had delivered to them earlier. It was a gift from the Baylor Medical Center of Dallas, solicited by my daughter, Krista, and brought when she and Jonlyn came for their summer vacation. We invited his lab technician to our hospital to learn some other simple lab tests. These tests make diagnosis more accurate thus saving valuable medicine.

Our team prepared a nice supper, jungle Karen dishes that I was not familiar with but enjoyed. After some time talking, I felt like it was bedtime. No radio, TV nor lights, so why not? After eight PM it was dead quiet so there was no trouble sleeping. It was still pitch black when I woke to house noises at five o'clock. When I got up I saw one of Gae Plau's, I guess about a third-grader, was doing her lessons by candlelight. In a few minutes another child was heard repeating his lessons over and over.

The Burmese Karens have been interested in education since the missionaries helped to lead them out of animism. Kateeta has a primary school, middle school, and recently added a high school which has five hundred students, many coming from other areas to study. Then there is a Bible Academy with sixty students enrolled in a three year course of study. It is not unusual to find a Karen who has a perfect command of English. When we moved from central Thailand to work up on the Kwai River, a Thai friend offered to go with us to help with the move. After we had gotten settled into our new house, he went out to see the village there (Sangklaburi). On his tour he met an

Krista and Jonlyn on the Salween River ready for a village health trip 1994.

Krista preparing an immunization at village health clinic.

elderly Karen who was a graduate of Sandhurst Military Academy in the UK, then another Karen with a degree from a university in India, and a few others. When he returned, Nancy overheard him telling our cook (in Thai), "These people up here speak better English than these farangs!" (referring to us with our southern accent).

We set up shop in the church which was adjacent to the primary school. Dr. Tamlasay's nurses were there to give the immunizations. We had already trained them, and they were happy to do the job under the supervision of our nurses. While that was going on, Dr. Tamlasay, Prechai, and myself went next door to an empty school room to discuss the health program. I presented my idea of organizing a program with the village support. Dr. Tamlasay had some suggestions, but by and large agreed that he would have to discuss the matter with the headman, Gae Plau.

A lighter than usual turnout ended the clinic early. This was our third immunization trip (DPT, polio, and tetanus for pregnant women). The light attendance was explained to me by Dr. Tamlasay: A meeting was called by the headman after our last visit to discuss financial support. No one in the meeting had any suggestions, so the headman came up with an idea. An offering box was prepared and placed in front of the clinic so that anyone could make an offering if they wished. This little box had frightened many people away. I really didn't think much of the idea, but at least he had tried something.

The hospital was the site of our afternoon clinic. It was way back on the other side of the hill, out of range of Burmese artillery. It was a little wooden building with a wood floor which served as the beds as well. The roof was made from Tung leaves stitched together with bamboo. The three or four patients he had were scooted aside for the clinic. The events proceeded as they had in the morning. Dr. Tamlasay took the opportunity to inform me of his problems. He had no salary, couldn't charge for medicine or services, frequently lacked essential medicines, and the people wanted instant cures for for their month old ailments, etc. Moreoever, the leaf roofs last only two years. He and his family had to walk two to three hours to collect the leaves, carry them back home, and stitch them together. I thought to myself, "A genuine jungle doctor."

While he was talking, I kept thinking of how to get these people organized or motivated for a health program. I was sent out here to try to develop a rural health program of some kind. About all I have to show for my efforts is that I have shut down most of the village health programs that existed because they weren't doing any good.

Then an idea hit me. Why not try to get some of those Bible Academy students to be paramedical workers who could be trained as village health organizers? Assign two or three of them to each of the seven districts of the village. Let them teach some simple health concepts such as the value of immunizations, etc., and let them be responsible for announcing the dates of the immunization clinics. I can really make things sound good in my own mind, and the more I thought about it, the better it sounded. After all, Jesus taught his disciples by going all over the country while teaching them and doing good things. This would be a good opportunity for the Academy to teach some practical Christianity. Dr. Tamlasay thought it was a good idea, but we must talk to the headmaster of the Academy.

So, after the clinic (101 baht or 4 dollars in the box) we made our way over to the nearby academy to see the headmaster if available. We attempted to present our idea. He listened receptively, made some inquiries, then agreed that there might be some possibilities in the plan. Then he wanted to know what we could do for the health of his students. I explained how we were helping the hospital, the lab equipment, etc, but that didn't seem to be sufficient for him. In the end I surmised that he was more interested in getting something out of us than in working with us, so my spirit hung low as I made my way back to the guest house. Another of my bright ideas.

Dr. Tamlasay and I stopped to see the headman of the village to discuss some of my ideas about the health plan. He was home, so we started with some introductory remarks. Before we could get to the meat of the matter, some visitors interrupted the conversation. A boatload of preachers from down the river had just arrived. Soon I discovered that they were the vanguard of a hoard of two hundred Karen preachers who were to descend on Kateeta from all over the Karen Free State for the weekend for an evangelisitic conference. Knowing the appetite of preachers, I though to myself that if this place wasn't poor before, it sure will be by the time the week is over. I didn't get a chance to talk to Gae Plau again about health matters. I guess that's just as well.

As usual I woke before dawn, so lay there thinking. Why could not there be someone here like Somyint, a Karen evangelist we had known from the Kwai area? She had come from Burma to be a missionary in a remote area. She came to our hospital to take a health course, then invited our village health team to her non-Christian village. Everytime we went, she had a nice meal prepared for us. Within a few months those children were as healthy as children anywhere, and we always collected our modest fee from an obviously poor village.

It was still dark, but a neighbor child that must have been about weaning age began to announce his discomfort to the neighborhood. His cry was a cross between a moan and a whine, and with it he effectively proclaimed his dislike for the village of Kateeta. At least that is how I interpreted it with the mood I was in that morning. Preachers were sleeping all over the floor around me, but I decided to get up anyway.

The sun was up, and I walked to the edge of the river bank. The pastor of Kateeta Church and a visiting preacher were standing there, so I joined them. Kids and ducks were running all over the place. I asked the pastor where he lived. He pointed to the nearby house, then started naming his children. The yard was full of them, and they were all his. I thought to myself that if he were as good at proclaiming as procreating he must have a growing church.

Breakfast was over and the boat was waiting. I was the last one in the procession. On the way to the boat we passed by a gourd vine up on a trellis built over a little ravine. I had come with hopes and ideas that would give a better life to Kateeta, but not much had come of it. I felt like a jungle Jonah. That gourd vine looked so inviting that I believe I could have sat under it and sulked all day, enjoying every minute of it. Prechai yelled from the boat. When I got to the boat he asked me what I had been looking at. I acted as if I didn't hear him, for I couldn't translate those thoughts into Thai.

J. Freeman

30 October 1993

Dear Friends,

Last night wasn't a good night for sleeping. A Thai market town is one of the noisest places on earth. Maesariang doesn't quite measure up to Tap Sai, the little town where we lived while working with the Cambodian refugees, but it comes close. You would think that they would all sleep at night but no, I think they sleep in shifts. Mabe there are not enough beds to go around.

Anyway the intercom called me at two AM so had to go down to the Hospital. A pretty young wife was lying on the bed with both eyes blacked and filled with tears. Her drunk soldier-husband had beaten her up. For no reason but that he was stronger than she was. Women have a tough time in the world. Those who should look after them and protect them find ways to abuse them. We got her to bed, then heard a squalling down the hall. Saiyon the nurse invited me to check the OB patient and sure enough she was about ready. We went to the delivery room and for a change had an uneventful delivery. A pretty little girl came out, and the mother was all smiles for that was what she wanted. I thought to myself she doesn't know what she is in for. Come to think of it, it wasn't altogether uneventful. The lights went out in the middle of the delivery and there were no emergency lights in the room-seems like nothing ever goes smoothly in our little hospital, and how everyone gets well and goes home is still a mystery to me. I was about to get heated up at not having light when it occurred to me that babies are born all the time without much light so I cooled down and used my knowledge of braille. Lights finally came, courtesy of the night watchman and our emergency generator.

When that was over I walked out to go home and noticed some candles and torches in front of the hospital. Being naturally curious I walked over to inquire into the nature of this three AM display. It turned out that the cause for all the celebration of the past few nights is the Buddhist holiday of "Auk Pansaa" which is the time of the priests leaving the monestary. The Buddhist young man is not "suk"(mature) until he has spent at least three months in the priesthood. There is a lot of meritmaking in this process with the most going to the parents as a result of the son entering the priesthood.

I stood there in the street and discussed the occasion with a friend for a few minutes. Then I mentioned that we had just had our own little "auk" (coming out) ceremony in the hospital, only it was a little girl instead of a male. He thought that was amusing so rushed over to tell another friend.

The streets were still dark from the power outage, but I noticed that there were a lot of lights down the street. I went on down to investigate. Little booths were set up on both sides of the street as far as I could see. Each had a little palmbranch arch over the table. The affair was lighted with candles, paper lanterns and resinous pine torches. The tables were laden with various kinds of food packages, little sacks of rice, canned fish, sweets etc. I was told that the priests would be along shortly and the food was offerings for them, this being more of the merit making of the "auk pansaa."

This middle of the night ceremony was something I had never seen elsewhere in Thailand. One of the families informed me that this was performed here in Maesariang only. Whole families were out mingling around the booths, except the babies. The youngest I observed were those old enough to play with fireworks. I had to be careful of all the explosions as I made my way down the street. Suddenly a huge starburst errupted a few blocks away. When it was gone I noticed a full moon, this figures, as all Buddhist occasions are by the moon. I had a good time talking to the different families, some patients, and some shop keepers.

A sudden stirring made me look around. The adults were gathering up their food baskets and lining up on one side of the road. Down the street in the direction of the hospital there came a single file of yellow robed priests, shaved heads and bare feet. An empty bench on the opposite side of the street invited my tired body so I sat down to watch. Dozens of the priests came by silently with their begging bowls in their hands. The folks picked a small food package from their baskets, lifted it respectfully to their face then deposited it in the bowl. A package for each priest. Some young men were pushing carts along for the priests to empty their full bowls into. This process went on all night for three nights so that would be quite a bit of booty. It reminded me of halloween and the "trick or treaters." I thought of all the money flowing to make merit but when it comes to paying for a life saved in the hospital it is often like getting blood out of a turnip.

There on the bench I thought as an endless procession of monks passed and the children continued to set off fireworks. Religion is all too often full of form but short on substance. All this show and what for? Of course, in Christianity we are guilty of this also. Stay awake in church now and then and see how much substance you get from some sermons. But this was an interesting celebration. This was a bit like Christmas (decorations), Fourth of July (fireworks), and Halloween (collections) all rolled into one. We had something like this when we were in Saudi Arabia. They called it Rammadan. That was a month when they fasted and slept all day then feasted and played all night.

It wouldn't be polite to leave at this time so I kept sitting and thinking. Buddha spent his whole life searching for the basic substance of truth and in the end offered as his supreme wisdom that the way to enlightenment is through complete suppression of desire, all kinds of desire. When enlightened, the person is entitled to Nirvana that "celestial" state that he could not describe except in negatives, "it is not that and it is not this etc." He formulated some good rules as well.

Jesus came to give truth, the truth that when received had the power to transform desire into a spring of living water. In Buddhism desire is suppressed-well, not exactly since there is this huge sex industry here. In Islam the object of desire, the woman, is shrouded in a black sack (another way of degrading women), with the understanding that desire will be free to run rampant unless the object is covered.

Again the words of Jesus, "Ye shall know the Truth and the Truth will set you free" (John 8:32). It dawned on me that it must be four o'clock and that tomorrow I wouldn't be able to sleep all day so I headed for home and bed as the city lights came on.

Sincerely,
J. Freeman

4 November 1993

HUEY PAA (FOREST STREAM VALLEY)

It was November third and we had surveyed the villages of Mae Sawlo, Mae Sawlo Tai, Huey Mu and Huey Mu Nua all in the hills above Kom Koi. Most of the Karen hills are beautiful and that area was no exception. I felt pleased at what we had accomplished but saddened at what we learned. Infant mortality rate was near forty to fifty percent, they were members of the "flat earth society" and no one had ever been to their villages to tell them the good news of Christ. Neh Geh had suggested that we use our last day to visit a couple of Sgaw Karen villages north of the main Chiang Mai-Maesariang highway. So, after completing a portrait of the headman in his official headman's uniform, complete with battle ribbons, we packed our gear and headed north.

It was about noon when we turned off the main highway at the large sign announcing the Mae Hong Song Province(the one we live in). We followed a well used dirt road cut from the steep hills which paralleled the Huey Paa. Neh Geh told me that the road had originally been cut for a timber road even before the main highway. I believed him for there was not a timber grade tree in sight on the whole ride. Terraced rice fields stairstepped their way up the narrow valley. The valley narrowed in places allowing only the small clear water stream to pass, but the fields could be seen in most places, some areas containing several acres of fields. Small terraced fields were constructed in every conceivable place-testimony to many years of habitation. Every little side "huey" (valley or ravine) had the terraces as far as we could see.

During rice planting season, I had written someone, that rice cultivation was the most exotic form of agriculture and the sights of this day reaffirmed that impression. Our trip up the valley coincided with the peak of the harvest season. Everywhere the fields were golden with the ripe heads of grain some so heavy they were lying down. We stopped to watch as several people down below were cutting the rice by hand then tying it into sheafs left to dry behind them When the engine was turned off the quietness was disturbed by the rip-

Village scene near Salween River.

Slash and burn hillside and terraces ready for planting in Maesariang area.

Preparing a field for rice planting.

Planting rice.

Harvest time in rice field.

Threshing rice into basket. Note recovering slash and burn fields in background.

Winnowing the rice.

pling stream and birds singing. In the distance the cowbells, some of metal, bamboo or teak were making a melody. The sky was perfectly clear and a cool fall breeze blew over the hills, lush green, and the valley golden with ripe grain. I thought to myself that I had never been in a more beautifully tranquil place in all my life.

Baan Sut Huey Na was the first village we came to, and as it was past noon Prechai and Neh Geh were anxious to stop. This was a small village of sixteen houses all of them containing relatives as one man explained. Neh Geh quickly struck up a conversation with a friendly man, then invited himself to use his kitchen to cook up some Mama noodles for our lunch. The Karen for the most part are naturally friendly, and I suppose they enjoy strangers as a form of entertainment. We were invited up into the house where we sat and talked while Neh Geh prepared our lunch.

The eighty-year-old mother of the Paw Baan (man of the house) came in and caught my attention as she seemed so alert and pleasant. She had lived in this village all her life as had her parents and as far back as anyone else could remember. It was easy to understand why they never moved. It turned out that she was the local Maw Tam Yea, and according to her memory had delivered about one hundred babies. The only deaths were two stillbirths. No, she had never heard of any birth deformities. I was also interested in how she treated birth lacerations to the mother. She never bothered with them, and all healed without any problem. The mothers were all kept by the fire seven days without food proscriptions except pigmeat from uncastrated males was forbidden (it smelled). She usually received for her services a home woven skirt and a bowl of water of boiled herbs with which to wash her face.

I was curious as to know what was done with the placenta. That was placed in a bamboo cup tied up in a nearby tree of the family's choosing. Afterwards that tree was special and no one was allowed to bother it. If the baby became ill then the mother or the midwife would take an egg plus a handfull of boiled rice carried in a fold of their blouse and go to the tree. She would hit on the tree several times with a special bamboo stick to attract the spirit of the tree. About this time the Paw Baan got up went into another room and fetched a three-foot-long bamboo stick splintered on one end and with three notches

The local Maw Tam Yea (widwife) with two children she delivered.

on the other. After striking the tree gently she would make a motion with her cupped hand inviting the spirit to go back with her to the house. When at the house she would hit the post of the house several times, then go in hoping the "kwan" (spirit) would remain with the child. Prechai explained that other villages have variations of this interesting custom.

The Maw Tam Yea's husband had died five years ago so I inquired as to the cause of his demise. The last five years of his life he walked about all the time, wouldn't sleep, was angered easily, and then died because he wouldn't eat. His symptoms could have been caused by a stroke but it was the first time in Thailand that I had ever heard of someone with symptoms similar to Alzheimers's disease.

On inquiring as to the other diseases in the village the Paw Baan began to tell me of his cure for malaria. He had treated several and none had died; in fact, no one in his village had ever died from malaria. He had a little bush planted across the road, which after lunch he took us to see; from that plant he would get a root about six inches long. It would be folded in the middle with the ends trimmed off and thrown away. The other ends would be trimmed about one half inch and thrown into the fire. The remaining two pieces, about three inches long would be boiled. The water was then given to the patient to drink. It may be boiled several times with the water each time being given to the patient. It had a Karen name of Naw Po according to Prechai and Neh Geh.

I asked the man of the house if there were ceremonies concerning this rice harvesting season. There were none before planting, but after the harvest there would be a day of feasting to offer thanks to the spirits. This would consist of each house sacrificing a chicken, for curry, making homemade whiskey and eating some of the new rice. He seemed to be proud that his village didn't fear the spirits like those Pwo Karens in the Kom Koi area, but it seemed evident that they did believe in the spirits and offered sacrifices to them. They were Buddhist but had no temple. Buddhists have no god so it is common all over Thailand for people to offer gifts to the spirits on certain occasions.

Neh Geh came out with the noodles which we enjoyed. Then I sold several doses of worm medicine before bidding farewell. That

A village boy carrying his brother.

village appeared as poor as the others we had just come from by the looks of the houses, but there were earmarks of prosperity. The ease with which the Paw Baan turned loose money for worm medicine, a walk-behind paddy tractor under the house, the intelligent speech of the children-all spoke of prosperity (as well as the lush rice fields).

Slowly we made our way up the valley with me enjoying every second of the trip. After about thirty minutes I had to stop to take in the scenery. Two little boys and a half dozen cows had the road blocked. We got out and talked and looked. The older boy was about nine years and had a large machete in one hand. He had a snotty-nosed little brother of about five years. When we approached the older "wai'ed" (palms together in front of the face with slightly bowed head; the traditional Thai greeting) politely and gave the usual oral greeting, then the little one followed suit. I knew then that they had, at least the older, been under the influence of a Thai schoolteacher. I asked him if he enjoyed herding the cows. He answered honestly "no" by shaking his head. Then I asked him if he were teaching his little brother to be a good herder. He looked affectionately down at his little brother, and with a mix of a smirk and a grin bent over picked up a stick and scraped the snot off the upper lip of the little brother. I thought to myself that these kids were growing up in a paradise; what else could they want? The biggest problem they had could be cured with a little stick.

    I walked to the edge of the road to look almost straight down into the valley filled with rice fields. The happy talk and occasional laughter of a group of harvesters drifted up. Two other women were in another threshing area beating the sheafs of rice on a pole, a pile of rice at their feet. Opposite was another little ravine filled with stairstepping paddies of uncut rice. Up the valley could be seen the neat government school that I suspected but closed today for some reason. Other than the government school this scene could have been thousands of years old. Abraham's servants used the same methods in his day.

    We needed to survey another village so I reluctantly pulled myself away and on we drove. Neh Geh asked if we wanted to stop in Mae Lit. It was across the huey and for the most part obscured by a hill on which stood a newly constructed wooden church with a cross on it. Neh Geh went on to tell that it was a Catholic church but that there were about a halfdozen or so Baptists houses in the village as well. We passed it by as we had in mind another village at the end of the valley. The beauty of the valley continued to amaze me. A large patch of sunflowers for which this area is famous was in full bloom across the valley.

    Finally we arrived at the top of the valley and turned off the road to go up to Mae Lit Paa Kee, a small village that seemed on top of the world. This village had a small Buddhist temple as well as a Baptist church. The church was made of bamboo with grass roof and a red cross. It reminded me of the little church up on the Kwai that the villagers at Beke had built. The nonChristians in the village made fun of it and called it a chicken house. Nai Chert the church leader laughed about it, though; it didn't bother him. Anything for a laugh is OK with the Karens. This was a very simple structure but in front of the church where I stood two giant rubber trees (of the decorative type we have in our houses) framed it. I thought, "who needs a beautiful building when surrounded by God's own beauty such as in this place?" Neh Geh knew the people of the village, so we followed him on into the village of thirty houses.

Neh Geh informed us that a wedding was in progress in the house of one of the church members and that we were invited to the house. Neh Geh is a master at living off the land; moreover, food would certainly be served at the wedding so I knew that it would be futile to argue with him. Ducks, chickens and pigs littered the yard. A blue plastic water tap stood near the entrance, and I noticed a toilet just in back of the house constructed of bamboo, thatch with board floors. The government is big into water systems and toilets for the hilltribes now, but it was the missionaries years ago who began helping them with these projects.

Going into the house I glanced into the smoke darkened kitchen to the left to noticed a group of women around the dirt-filled fire box. They were still busy cooking over the open wood fire. We went to the right into a room filled with villagers. I had to ask who the groom was. It turned out that he was from Buri Ram in the Northeast part of Thailand who had been in this area building roads. He met this Christian girl and decided to stay. The ceremony was already over, so the bride was moving around. She was a very nice, strong looking girl. It seemed he had made a good choice.

Conversation was mostly in Sgaw Karen with some in Thai for the sake of the groom who didn't speak much Karen yet. Next thing I knew out came a Bible and hymn book which were presented to Neh Geh. He looked a minute or two for the right passage, then led in a song, which everyone knew, a sermon for the bride and groom was next. These Karens are a lot like the evangelical group I once visited in Romania called the Lord's Army. Any occasion where people are gathered together is an occasion for a song and a sermon. There I went to a Lord's Army wedding and during the reception the preaching went on for four and one-half hours while the bride and groom sat silently behind a table in front of the room. To his credit Neh Geh didn't preach too long.

Food was then brought out, so we ate to the health and happiness of the newlyweds. This was a rather informal affair. In the middle of it all I had a consult with the headman's wife about her visual problems, then sold several doses of worm medicine. I did some quick medical survey as well to learn of no childhood deaths in the village in ten years. Of four families I questioned, they had a total of twenty-five children with no deaths.

Much of the credit for the health of the village goes to the government health clinic and the school which have been there for several years. In addition is the water system and the toilet program. More recently a government agricultural station has been established, a part of the King's program for hilltribe development. I have observed also that in villages where there are Christians the health is better and the people are more progressive. Being slaves to the spirits as those in the Kom Koi area is certainly an impediment to progress.

As we left the village we could see in every direction the evening sun casting a blue haze silhouetting the distant hills, range after range. We passed hillside cabbage, bean, and corn fields. Finally at about sunset we came to Mae Ho and the little Catholic church where earlier I had come, at the invitation of our local Karen Catholic priest, to talk to a conference about medical problems. There we came to the main highway and finally on home.

J. Freeman

4 November 1993

HUEY MU KLANG

On the morning of November 4th after completing our work in Sawlo Tai we drove over to Huey Mu Klang a village of about sixty houses. This village had a new water system and was much like the other villages so I won't say anymore about that. On arriving we found that there is a governmment health station so we walked up the hill towards it as we had been told that the "doctor is in." About one hundred feet out of the village on the side of the road were some chicken feathers which was pointed out as a recent spirit sacrifice. It is common practice for the people in this area, after being treated in the hospital and I presusme other clinics as well, to feed the spirits. The ones who do this get well better according to one man from Mae Pae. But he admitted that one of his children died even after feeding the spirits. He had taken the child away from our hospital before we had completed our treatment.

We arrived at the health clinic, closed up tight, but with the doctor's (health worker) pickup in the yard. Then one of the villagers informed us that he was out sawing wood and explained that he had another "achiep" (profession) as well and that was getting lumber from the forest. We looked around the neat facility a minute then went back to find the headman.

The headman promptly showed up and was very accomodating in telling us strangers about his village. Among some of the things gleaned from our conversation: no school in the village, there is a midwife who according to him charges fifty to one hundred bhat per delivery, worms were abundant in the village, there were about 100 cows in the village, the women all had an abundant amount of jewlery as in other surrounding villages, several children, five or six, die each year and they were all in the under five age group.

I noticed that a half dozen of the children had plastic syringes with the needles attached, evidence of the government health clinic. Oral medications are usually distributed free from the health clinics but the most "powerful medicine" in this area comes from a shot and the people are willing to pay for this even if it is a worthless vitamin shot which is often the case. The last lecture in medical school in Memphis was a talk given by the ex-dean the subject being Medical Quackery. The most important lecture of the school saved for the last. As long as there are medics there will be quacks and we have our share in the States and many with an M.D. after their names.

The headman said that there was no opium users in his village but there were about ten in the sister village nearby over which he had responsibility as well. He wanted to know if there was anything that we could do to help. I said that I would like to go and have a look at the village so he willingly guided us to Huey Mu Nua a village of about fifty houses.

Again Huey Mu Nua was about like Huey Mu Klang but situated over a hillside. Of the three families I talked to there were twelve living children and thirteen that had died. We were escorted to a house with a sick nursing infant suffering from pneumonia. I left medicine for it but it was so sick that I doubt it lived. Of the remaining children that we saw in the village they looked rather healthy.

According to the headman there were about ten opium addicts in the village. These addicts would steal from others or sell their own belongings to suppoort their habit. We discussed ways the hospital could help but only if all of the addicts in the village would accept a cure at the same time and then outlaw opium from the village. He promised to do what was required but he was a young headman so doubted his ability in spite of his sincerity.

We met in this village, the father of the adopted daughter of the New Tribe Missionaries, the Richards. The mother had died in childbirth a couple years before. According to the custom in that area the newborn infant even if alive must be buried with the mother, the baby being placed under the dead mother. The Richards heard about the death and offered to take the infant who is now thriving. Just last month another such incident occured and on a visit to the village I saw the Richards with another infant rescued from such a fate. The father though refused to let the Richards keep the little girl and took it back to raise himself. It died before the month was out due to poor feeding practice.

We walked on to the end of the village where a man with a forge lived. He wasn't working on anything at the time but I noticed several new bamboo harvest baskets under his house an indication that he was a rather industrious individual. I asked him how much they sold for and was told a price of between three hundred and four hundred bhat. I haven't thought of a good reason to have one of them but sure am tempted to buy one.

We went on back to Huey Mu Klang and arrived there in time for me to take a bath before supper. I had missed by bath the day before so was anxious to try out the new water tap sitting in the middle of the village. Of course no one there had ever seen a farang take a bath in the middle of their village before so all eyes were watching. That was not the first time to bath in public but I'm still apprehensive that something may come loose and thus expose all my business.

Neh Geh and Prechai rustled around and got up some suppper then we sat around a candle and floor knothole (to spit through) and began the evening discussion. The subject of pees (spirits) came up first and the headman didn't seem to mind in the least admitting that he had never seen one, didn't know if they were large or small, tall or short, etc, but regardless he was certainly afraid of them. I tried to tell them about the Great Spirit that we served who instead of always being out to do us in, loves us and wants to give us the abundant life. I tried to draw them into a discussion along this line but was cut off by the headmen who said, "We don't think about these things too much. All we are interested in is trying to get enough rice to eat."

Prechai saw an opening so took the opportunity of trying to explain the Gospel to them. He hadn't started good when Neh Geh returned from his bath sat down and listened long enough to get the gist of the conversation. When he got started he kept going with his audience laughing bantering back and in general having a good time. Although it was all in Karen it sounded like some good teaching to me. He discussed Jesus, rice cultivation, the round earth for about two hours or until bedtime. So, that was Huey Mu Klang.

J. Freeman

13 December 1993

Dear friends,

Santa Claus came early this year and brought us some nice presents in the form of visitors from afar. Those of you who have ever lived in a remote area for a long time will readily appreciate how welcome friends can be.

When we were up on the Kwai we were in an even more remote area than we are now. Visitors were a contact with the outside world as well as a special form of "entertainment" to us. Mail came once or twice a month and telegrams informing us of a coming visitor usually came several weeks after the visitor had come and gone. Visitors there were especially welcome at the hospital since they were usually good blood donors. Those that we worked with were rather primitive and not inclined to shed their blood even for a loved one. One of the first salutations to a visitor was, "What is your blood type?"

Late one afternoon, a tired but rather distinguished gentleman appeared at our door and, in high-sounding British English, introduced himself and inquired about accommodations for the night, there being no public guest houses in the area. He looked and sounded interesting, so we invited him in. We discovered that he was an ex-prisoner of the Japanese who had survived the Death Railroad during World War II. After the war, Stanley returned to the U.K. where he studied law and was at that time sitting as judge (sheriff as they call it) in Inverness, Scotland. In addition to that he was a "Queen's Counsel" which didn't mean much to me, but being a country boy and jungle doctor, I was sufficiently impressed. This trip brought him to Kanchanaburi to retrace steps and memories of those war years.

Stanley and I went out to the remains of the railroad where he walked down the grade with teak and maidang (a hardwood) ties (sleepers) in place, many with spikes remaining from the days when the prisoners pounded them in. We happened upon a homemade still in a village. Stanley sipped a sample but declined to purchase a bottle; he said that it didn't quite compare to real Scotch. Then one day he went out with us on a village clinic which brought back memories of the diseases endured by the prisoners: malnutrition, diphtheria, chol-

Stanley beside a bombed out railroad car similar to the one which carried him and his buddies from Singapore to the Kwai River (photo 1974).

A village moonshine still which Stanley and I happened upon (1974).

era, chronic skin ulcers, beri-beri, etc. As he left, Stanley invited us to visit him in Scotland.

Furlough time came and Inverness was one of our stops on the way home. Stanley took us and the kids in his antique convertible (he still has it) to see the Loch Ness Monster. The kids saw the monster, but my imagination was not keen enough. I am sure it was there since Stanley assured me it was. I have been told that when a Scottish Sheriff states a fact, then one can stand on it. The children received a tour of the courtroom and a demonstration of the wig worn by Stanley while presiding.

In 1983, while we were working in Southwest Saudi Arabia on the edge of the Empty Quarter, Stanley appeared on our doorstep again. We had a good time running around over that rocky mountainous part of the Arabian peninsula. One day we decided to drive down to Najaran, a good-sized little city made of mud houses typical in that area. I had heard about the "Forbidden City" somewhere near Najaran that was off-limits to all us expatriates, except with a pass from the Prince of Najaran. Since we could not get a pass, we forgot about that interesting site. According to our sources, the "Forbidden City" was the ruins of a city of Christians which had been destroyed and massacred by Muslims.

Nancy had already taken a trip to that place, so Stanley and I took off alone in our old Peugeot station wagon. After driving around town and looking at the large palace belonging to the Prince of Najaran made entirely of mud, we decided to drive out in the country and see the farms. We drove a while, then noticed some ruins off to the right. We whipped off the road and hiked over to inspect the situation. Soon we were up on top of the large stone foundations, surveying what looked to be about ten or twenty acres of an ancient city, and wondering just what it had been. After a few minutes we noted a Toyota pickup kicking up sand as it flew toward us across the desert. Out jumped a slight Arab with his gutra headdress flying in the wind. He was waving his hands as he approached, yelling, "Mamnouh, mamnouh!" (forbidden, forbidden, in Arabic). I turned to Stanley and said, "By Jove, I think we have stumbled onto the 'Forbidden City'." We made profuse apologies as best we could and departed, content that we were not arrested and that we had seen the most interesting sight

Stanley at dinner in home of Ah Nu and Cristabelle who were in charge of student hostel in 1993 in Maesariang.

Last Christmas card from Stanley. He made this sketch while a prisoner on the Kwai River in 1943.

of Najaran.

    Stanley is a fascinating character. The next time we met was in York, England, where he showed us the sights in that historic old city. I was most impressed by the York Cathedral, well, not so much by that as what was underneath it. In order to strengthen the foundations, a few years ago they had to dig under the building where they discovered another set of ancient foundations. Every antique in the U.K. is preserved in place at great cost. Even Stanley, approaching eighty, is very well preserved. By the time we arrived in York, all of the excavation had been accomplished. Under the cathedral was a museum of an old Roman garrison, then under those relics was another set of Viking ruins, of course, predating the Roman era. Quite interesting.

This time in Maesariang Stanley and I didn't go out much but sat around and talked most of the time. We are getting too old to go around looking at all those ancient things. Stanley has taken a great interest in helping other ex-prisoners of the Death Railroad with pensions and compensations. He related a couple of stories from those days that I thought were interesting.

In one case, a question arose regarding the widow's pension. Was the early death due to smoking or did the stress of the POW years contribute? The man had never talked to anyone about his experiences, except to his daughter on one occasion. The daughter related his story. On one occasion the man had two close buddies who were seriously ill, one on the bed on either side of him. He had done all he could for them, but there was nothing to do with. Finally one of his buddies, in a fit of delirium, called out, "Bring me some food!" He thought a minute, then headed toward the mess area where he scrounged around and finally found some swill. A Japanese guard happened to spot him in the off-limits area and followed him back into their bamboo quarters. When the guard apprehended him, the man was standing, holding the bowl of swill, looking down at the lifeless buddy.

The Japanese took him, beat him unconscious, and when he awoke, he was in a bamboo cage four feet square and four feet tall. There he stayed for many days suffering until he was sufficiently broken in spirit that he finally offered the apology required to be set free from the cage. The legal case was settled in favor of the widow.

On another occasion, a young Japanese soldier was seen crawling back from the front lines near one of the British camps. One hand had been blown off and was poorly bandaged. As he was too weak to walk, he crawled, pulling his gear on the ground. A tall, gaunt British POW, who would not be taken for a man of a particularly kind nature, saw the scene. He walked over, knelt down and picked up that hated enemy soldier, cradled him in his arms and carried him to his destination to a barge at the river bank. He crossed the river on a bamboo pole foot bridge and waited on the other side. When the barge was pulled across he again picked up the young, suffering lad and carried him to the truck, waiting to evacuate the wounded. Then he reached into his precious tobacco pouch, rolled a cigarette, lit it, and put it to the mouth of his enemy.

"And His name shall be called Emanuel which means God with us." Whether friend or foe, "God so loved the world that He have His only begotten Son that whosoever believes on Him shall have everlasting life." John 3:16

MERRY CHRISTMAS!!

Love and Peace,
John & Nancy Freeman

24 December 1993

Dear Krista,

   Ever since we came this time, we have been looking forward to a visit to our old Kwai River Christian Hospital. The visit came to pass last week. The thing that impressed us was the many friends who are still working in the hospital who were there when we left sixteen years ago. Waloseng, the gardener, is the only one who didn't move to the new location with the hospital.
   You, being almost a nurse by now, will appreciate that the person there who made the greatest impression on me is Ebra, our Karen nurse. She had begun working in the hospital when Dr. Roy Meyers was there. When we reopened the hospital in 1974, she was living there, so rejoined our staff. She is still working there, and it was a pleasure to work along with her again while we were there for our short visit. When we were there, she was the head nurse, but technically she never held the title since she was never allowed to sit for the Thai licensing exam. But as far as I was concerned, she could do any job in the hospital, and would do it anytime necessary without complaint. She could run the outpatient clinic, and took care of the inpatients when I was away. I consider such a person a head nurse.
   Ebra was trained in the Moulmein Christian Hospital in Burma during the time when missionaries were still allowed there. American doctors and nurses were there still running the hospital and nursing program. If most of the graduates were like Ebra, then they had a tremendous program. Mom is always talking about how important it is to have a professional attitude as a nurse. If you want a perfect example of that, just go and follow Ebra around. Three words can best describe her personality: calm, cool, and confident. She quietly goes about her duties with a perfect mix of grace and skill. I don't know how anyone could learn all that, so I must conclude that she was born with it.
   If Ebra ever lost her cool, I don't think I knew about it except with Hippo, Patrick's nephew, who was brought in semi-comatose one day. All the meager diagnostic tests that we had at our disposal were of no help in pinning down the cause of his illness, which rapidly developed

into hepato-renal failure and a deep comatose state. Hippo bled from almost everywhere, and we pumped blood into him in an attempt to keep him in blood-balance. For several days I wouldn't have bet a nickel on him, but then one day Ebra thought he might be a little better. The next day he was sitting up in bed flirting with the nurses. Ebra finally had to come down on him, but she did it in a nice way.

Hippo's illness was interesting in that I thought of everything, including leptospirosis (endemic in our area), but never was sure until years later when I read a textbook description of Weil's Disease, a severe complication of leptospirosis. That description fit Hippo so perfectly that I am sure now that was his problem. Patrick came by for a visit while we were there and asked me if I remembered Hippo. "Of course," I said, "I cannot ever forget him." Then he told me that he had been killed. It seems that he was working for the Karen National Union in the intelligence department. According to Patrick, the Karens were responsible for his death, so Hippo must have been suspected of some kind of double-dealing.

Ebra was a quick thinker and intelligent as well. You just don't expect to find people of her caliber out in the jungle. Once she called me over to see a young man with a seizure. When I arrived, the seizure was over and the patient in postseizure unconscious state. Ebra had a scalpel in her hand and explained that she had noticed an abscess on his leg and decided to go after it while he was out, and thus save a little time and money on numbing the area. Now that is taking advantage of an opportunity.

Nurses have kept me out of trouble on several occasions, and not only me but the patient as well. We had a woman from Takanun once who had come down with diabetes insipidus. Other than drinking a tub full of water each day and, of course, getting rid of an equal amount, I couldn't find anything else wrong with her except that she was pregnant. My jungle consults (old textbooks) didn't help me much with the situation. I decided that we might be able to help her by giving her some pitocin. Ebra asked if we should do that with her being pregnant. I agreed that wasn't such a good idea and decided to wait and see what happened. She went ahead and delivered a healthy baby.

Another impressive thing about Ebra is her language skills. When she came to Thailand, she had a fluent knowledge of English in addition to her native Karen and Burmese. Now she speaks Thai very well along with the local dialect of Karen which is different from her native Karen. She wasn't very good with the Mon language when we were there, but now she does a good job with it.

Life has not always been kind to Ebra. At times she has been harassed because of not having Thai citizenship. She cannot return to visit her home or relatives in Burma because of working in a Karen National Union controlled area. Travel in Thailand is not allowed, so she remains there in the area remote from what we call civilization, but actually it is much more civilized than most places in the world. Sometimes God tempers our lives by these difficulties. At any rate, thousands of suffering souls with no other medical facilities available have been touched by Ebra with her kindness and compassion. She is what I call a real Jungle Jewel.

And so it is, Krista, that Ebra has brightened one little corner of the world, and you will, I am sure, find a place that needs brightening as well.

Love,
Dad

24 December 1993

Dear Jonlyn,

Mom and I just returned from the Kwai River Christian Hospital. It was Mom's first visit there since we left in 1977. I enjoyed the work in the hospital, to see and experience what is going on there. On our trip to the Kwai, I happened to read a review of a book written by Søren Kierkegaard by a Mr. Poole. Mr. Poole thought that Kierkegaard's Christianity was totally irrelevant, so he admonished the reader to "Skip God" when studying the philosophy of Kierkegaard. Skip God?

A lot of changes had, of course, taken place in the sixteen years since we left. The hospital is in a new location necessitated by the flooding caused by the new dam. The forest and the jungles are almost completely gone now, being replaced by rubber tree plantations and bamboo orchards. That is the first time I have ever seen bamboo cultivated! Sangklaburi is a thriving little city now, beginning to be a tourist Mecca.

The hospital is a beehive of activity these days and quite a contrast from the sleepy, slow pace that I remember when it sat on the bank of the Rantee River. The thing that pleased me the most was seeing all of the old hospital workers still at their duties. Of course, new ones had been added since the place has become much busier. Dr. Keith, a retired doctor now filling there, left for a much-needed break as soon as we arrived, so we had a working visit.

One of the first patients I admitted was a severely emaciated man, so weak that he was not able to walk or talk. He looked like the Japanese Death Railroad POW's, or more recently, those from the Serb concentration camps. He had been dumped at the Burmese border by the Thai police after a four-month internment. His crime that, as a Burmese national, he had worked in Thailand and was on his way back to Burma with his hard-earned pay. He was arrested, all his valuables confiscated, then left to molder in prison. He was given the right to telephone and write friends in order to appeal for more money which would, of course, enrich his captors more. We found that he also had severely advanced tuberculosis.

The above problem is so prevalent that one of the refugee relief organizations has opened a "half-way house" where the victims of Thai jails can be cared for while regaining their strength. Many of the women have severe traumatic stress syndromes. We visited the house and were surprised to find that Paw Lu Lu, one of our old village health trainees, was in charge. Well, it seems that many of the police here in Thailand have taken Mr. Poole's advice. They have skipped God.

One day another old friend showed up at the hospital for a visit. Patrick and I had worked together on some development projects, so we had some old times to talk over. He was the one who wrote and composed the music for a going-away song at our departure in 1977. He and his little "choir" stood in front of the house and sang while he played the guitar. Patrick told of the sad plight of the Burmese on the Tavoy area of Burma. Men were being forced into service for the government or the army; then the wives were forced to be bedmates for soldiers while their husbands worked. Just the other day I read in the paper that two hundred malnourished Karens had escaped from their Burmese army slave-masters and fled into Thailand. Those men had been used as porters by the Burmese army, which is very common. The Burmese, it seems, know how to "Skip God" as well.

It was about forty years ago when I was studying at the University of Texas. I remember some of my fellow students discussing Kierkegaard and his philosophy at that time, but the catch-phrase then was "God is dead." That made quite a stir at the time. Whether you say "God is dead" or just "Skip God" it probably makes no difference. Almost two generations have passed since I was there at UT and it seems that many are doing just that.

At our last breakfast up on the Kwai, we were eating with Dr. Keith Dahlberg, his wife, a visiting Family Practice resident, and his wife. In our discussion, Nancy and I told of an AIDS Day parade, here in Maesariang, in which we took part, along with others from our hospital. Nancy was embarrassed when she translated her Thai poster which said, "Always wear a condom." We bemoaned the fact that our Christian hospital did not encourage Christian morality in sex. Our resident friend objected that such would be imposing our own idea of morality onto a different culture.

To this family practice resident I gave an experience from our Maesariang hospital. A young mother had just given birth. Her AIDS screening test was positive. The husband was tested and his blood was also positive. We had to inform this mother that she would not be able to breast feed her newborn infant. Of course, this was a death sentence to the mother as well. Now, according to the studies I read, the Thai males visit prostitutes to the tune of ninety-five percent. My question to the young resident was, "Is there morality involved in that situation? And if there is morality, then should this not extend to all cultures?"

I had observed the young doctor in the hospital as he had given conscientious and selfless care to the patients. He was basically an honest person, so he admitted that the situation given above did, indeed, involve morality, but he hastily beat a retreat into the amoral reasoning instilled in his generation by our educational system and modern media. Basically he believed that morality-sexual morality was simply a figment of one's imagination.

For the past two generations, Americans have been busy at the amoral task of creating a vast subculture of fatherless citizens who are now the poor, the criminals, the drug users and terrorizing the country. Well, Mr. Poole, we have skipped God in America and look at the results!

So, Jonlyn, beware of philosophers with their fancy arguments and nebulous reasoning. The search for Truth is not hard to find IF you really want it.

Love,
Dad

25 December 1993

Dear Lloyd and Kerry,

    Here it is Christmas day and it would be nice to be there with all you kids. Here I am looking out the window as the cool winds rustle a large clump of bamboo in Thra Thunu's yard next door and, in the background the range of mountains separates our little valley from the Salween River valley and Burma.

    While we were up visiting (and working) in the Kwai River Christian Hospital we had a good visit with Kru(teacher) Boonchom and his wife Rebecca. Rebecca is still working as a nurse aid in the hospital as before when we were there. You may remember Kru Boonchom as he was your first-grade teacher there for several months. Mom had decided to let you try a dual schooling, in Thai Christian school there and home schooling in English as well. You dutifully went to school daily with your little uniform but it lasted only three or four months. For some reason things just didn't work out, so a first-grade dropout. But don't feel lonely for that as Krista was a kindergarten dropout as well, that is from Mom's home kindergarten. Kru Boonchom was a very kind and gentle person as are all Karens, but their teaching methods are a bit different.

    Our little Christian school there had some real problems while we were there as I remember, well actually I have tried not to remember. Getting qualified teachers to work in remote jungle areas in Thailand was almost impossible. We hadn't been there long before I was put on some kind of mission committee and it seemed that every time I turned around another crisis had developed in the school. I was still licking wounds from an unpleasant experience prior to moving there so was not inclined to get involved in other problems.

    There was a head teacher at one time who had a drinking problem. He had been reminded several times that drunkenness was not in keeping with his status. Finally he was given his last warning--one more time and you are out. Some of the other teachers who also had similar inclinations as the head teacher got wind of the warning. I suppose that they surmised that if the head teacher was gone then the position may be open to one of them so a conspiracy was hatched. The head teacher was invited to a party with a nice meal. When everybody was in a good mood a bottle was produced and spirits issued forth. The head teacher smelled a rat and therefore refused to imbibe. The teachers kept up the pressure, of course, by drinking themselves and in the end they were all drunk. Some kind of fracus resulted which brought the affair to the attention of the mission committee.

On another occasion an evil spirit brooded over the school and for what reason I don't recall. Late one night Emilie Ballard knocked on the door to inform me that there was a riot at the school. Since I was the chief riot control officer it fell my duty to inspect the situation. On arrival at the school at the other end of the compound the teachers were in the process of ransacking the school. A bonfire had already been lit and the next lighting on the agenda was the school itself. Somehow Emilie and I managed to get things under control and the building was saved. Such things were so regular that if I had had anything to say about it, I would have closed the school down.

There was another force at work in the school at that time and that was Kru Boonchom. He was a young man at that time who had been recruited to teach the first grade. His family was Christian living in the Chiang Rai area far to the north of Sangklaburi. The significant thing about Kru Boonchom was that he was a Christian in his heart, not only in name. He had left his home and family to go to a distant part of Thailand in order to teach but more than that to share the gospel of Christ to a people very few of whom believed in Christ. These people he came to serve were fellow Karens but of another dialect so he had to learn their language as well.

When I think of Kru Boonchom I am reminded of Abraham who left his homeland to go to a place God had called him. God had promised Abraham that he and his descendants would be a blessing to others. I think that Boonchom had first a firm commitment to Christ and to follow Him; arriving at Sangklaburi he developed a vision of what God had for him to accomplish. He quietly worked in the school and among the teachers in the manner of the yeast in bread that Jesus talked about.

So, what did we find when we returned after sixteen years? The school of one through the seventh grade has 450 students. Kru Boonchom is still there, the manager Kru Prasit is still there, and the head teacher, newly arrived when we left is still there. The school has produced several nurses for the hospital and a Karen doctor, a school graduate, will begin work in the hospital in a year or two. I inquired of Kamput my helper in the out-patient department one day as to his origins. From Chdengcheng he replied, and informed me that he was in the school and hostel when I was there. I didn't remember. "You should," he replied, "You took out my appendix when you were here."

Kru Boonchom was also the pastor of a little church in the Beke area not far from Chedengcheng. That church and members moved when the dam was built to the area near the hospital now. We went to the church on Sunday and heard Kru Boonchom preach. It is a larger church now and a better building that the bamboo "chicken coop" they had before. His sermons are still simple as a first grade teacher would have it and straight from the Bible reflecting his basic farmer-hunter instincts.

It is interesting what a Christian can do when he has commitment, vision and patience.

Love,
Dad

Christmas 1993
Dear friends,

Again it is the time to think of the birth of Christ and of the various animals that he was associated with. Those of us who are jungle doctors can appreciate this since animals are a part of everyday life. When we were up on the Kwai, it was not uncommon to see an elephant or oxcart pulled in front of the hospital with a patient. Waloseng asked me one day if the man who had been in the hospital for the bear-clawed face had ever paid his bill. I told him I did not know but would check. The man was from Waloseng's village which he intended to visit shortly, and since the bear-claw patient had plenty of cows, Waloseng, our gardener, would collect the debt. Later one Sunday I was awakened from a nap by a message from Waloseng requesting the hospital boat. The cow would have to be swum across the Songkalia River. That was done and we were in the cow business.

Someone was always stopping by, trying to give or sell me some kind of wild animal since they knew I had a passel of children. There was always a dog under the waiting room bench, and in quiet times chickens would wander through the waiting room. Speaking of chickens, I am reminded of a village clinic trip to the Beke area. I was sitting in the middle of a house holding a clinic with the house full of patients and villagers, all sitting on the floor, so I didn't pay much attention to a chicken that flew through the house now and then. I did notice though, when it landed in the lap of a patient sitting a short distance from me. He gave it a heave and it flew on out the front of the house which had no wall. At the end of the clinic I got up to stretch my legs and looked over in a large rice bin. There was a nest with about a dozen eggs. How they got those chickens to fly in the back, lay their eggs, then fly out the front, I never understood. That was handy for the cook.

Our animals here in Maesariang are all of smaller varieties. A small flock of black chickens graze regularly in the yard and occasionally ventures inside. One stately old rooster from across the street struts over now and then. He is a pet and thinks he owns the place the way he tries to intimidate those he meets. There is a set of roof cats that will occasionally come down to earth. I have never seen any rats or mice, so I leave them alone, but I would feel more kindly toward them if they developed a healthy appetite for cockroaches. I'm amazed at the endless variety of dogs who wander through. It must be the canine Grand Central Station. I never recognize any of them, except Pisut's red dog. Pisut is one of our night watchmen

Animals fascinate me, I suppose because as a child we had a backyard farm. When we moved from Arkansas to Rockport, Texas, we pulled a trailer with a jersey heifer in it. At one filling station she kicked a slat out of the chicken coop, and it wasn't long before Mom and all of us kids were chasing Rhode Island Reds all over the premises. Well, the heifer grew up and Mom milked it all through World War II, so we had as much milk, butter, and eggs as we needed. It was my job to take the cow each day to a different vacant lot to be staked and grazed. I think that milking was a time of meditation for Mom. She tried to teach me how once, but I couldn't seem to get the hang of it.

A few years ago while we were over on the Cambodian border doing some kind of survey, I saw something in a jungle that I will never forget. The ward of the hospital had a dirt floor, leaf-thatch roof and a half wall, no doors, of course. The young rebel medical worker was showing us their patients. We came to one bed, actually a small wooden platform raised off the ground. A young mother was sitting on one end, holding a healthy looking premature infant, while on the other end was the father, sitting cross-legged, holding a fuzzy puppy which seemed to have more attraction than his newborn. Tied to one leg of the bed was a domesticated variety of jungle chicken, maybe for supper. About that time, two three hand pigs ran through the ward squealing, in one door and out the other.

Jesus would have been right at home in that little jungle hospital, for he was born in similar circumstances. It was no accident that He was born in the midst of poverty. He was born to be vulnerable to all our human frailties. It is written that He was acquainted with all kinds of grief. He also calls us to live that same kind of life, vulnerable and acquainted with grief. His greatest promise: that He would be with us-- EMANUEL

Merry Christmas,
John & Nancy Freeman

26 December 1993

Dear Andrew,

The other day while visiting and working up at the Kwai River Christian Hospital and old patient and friend showed up in the clinic. I think that Nai Chert came more to see me but we eventually got around to examining his back which was keeping him from working. As I looked over his chart there was my noted from 1975 describing his tooth abscess.

It was that tooth abscess that brought Nai Chert back to the hospital about a year later when we were making plans to build a bridge across the Rantee River to connect the hospital and surrounding village with the main part of Sangklaburi. That tooth had long healed but he wanted to know if it would be possible for him to work on the bridge in order to pay the medical bill left over from that abscessed tooth. Nai Chert was a farmer from the Beke area and was a blacksmith in his spare time. At that time I didn't know him very well and had forgotten about him and his talents. In an instant I realized how valuable he would be in helping build the eighty foot long span of the bridge which would be constructed of railroad rails left from the Death Railroad. At that time I had only one other person to help and he was a carpenter with no experience in steelwork and for that matter neither had I. So Nai Chert turned out to be one of my chief engineers for the project.

Now you may wonder at my use of the word engineer for a blacksmith but in the old days blacksmithing was a prerequisite for an engineering degree. Granddad Freeman used to talk about his smithing course while in his first year engineering at the University of Arkansas. First he had to make his own forge tongs. Another assignment was to make a two-inch diameter steel ball within so many thousandths of an inch tolerance. To do this he had to calculate how much steel to cut from a two-inch square steel bar. Well, he never finished his engineering degree as he quit to go and "fight the Kaiser" in World War I.

Nai Chert had an engineers eye in addition to his smithing skills and if he had been exposed to education I'm sure he would have made an excellent engineer. He and a helper with a little charcoal forge straightened out several bent and twisted forty foot rails damaged from WW II American bombing of the railroad. Then he and Hlaing, the carpenter, began cutting and fitting and when they were finished the bridge was exactly like the blueprints that the Mile-Hi Engineering firm from Denver had sent. That process took the better part of a year so we developed a close friendship.

Nai Chert was quite a hunter as well and one day just before we left for furlough he stopped by and told about his most recent hunting trip. He had seen about every wild animal known to exist in that area including tapirs, wild cows, several kinds of deer, elephants etc. That whetted my appetite to see what he had described but it was too late to make that trip. He was to have been our guide to that wild animal park in 1981 when you, Lloyd, I and Philip and Paul made our jungle expedition. Nai Chert was off looking after his sick mother so he sent his son along in his place. As you remember we didn't see anything but a couple of hornbills and the fish they caught and salted to take back home.

We were invited to Nai Chert's home for supper one night while we were up there last week. After a tasty Karen meal we got to talking about the jungle. He insisted that the animals are still out there but it would take a long trip to get to them. He then told of his encounter with a tiger. It was about dusk when he noticed something strange on a ledge beside the trail. He bent over to get a closer look and followed the unusual object upwards wondering just what it was. Suddenly he realized that he was looking directly into the face of a large tiger sitting there on its haunches. In an instant he was wondering where to shoot the animal in the heart or head. He chose the head in order to keep it from biting him in case it sprang at him. He made the right decision and took the animal back home and gave it to neighbors.

Come to think of it that may be where that dried tiger meat came from that was given to us when we first moved up there. It was a time of meat scarcity as all the pigs and cows had died of a disease. Mom didn't know how to prepare dried tiger meat of course so we finally asked Olivia about it. She took it and fixed it and you kids thought it was the best thing you had eaten in a long time. As the Esso commercial at that time, "We had a tiger in every tank."

After we had moved away from Sangklaburi I had wondered just why Nai Chert and his family had moved from Chiang Rai to that area. So, after his animal tales we asked him. Kru Boonchom his younger brother had gone to Sangklaburi first in order to teach at our Christian School. During the vacation period Kru Boonchom went back to Chiang Rai where he asked Nai Chert to move to Sangklabui also saying that he could not stay there alone away from all his family. He went on to tell Chert that there were very few Christians in Sangklaburi and he wanted Chert to come help him as he sought to teach and spread the Gospel.

Nai Chert thought and prayed about the request many days then decided to heed his younger brother's "Macedonian Call". A missionary partnership was formed which still exists today with the older brother supporting the younger, Kru Boonchom as he teaches and pastors a growing church there.

Land prices have recently skyrocketed around Chaing Rai so Nancy asked him if he had ever regretted moving to Sangkla. His eyes twinkled as a smile covered his face, "Never have I regretted the move or doing anything God asked me to do."

Love,
Dad

30 December 1993

Dear friends,

   During the middle of December Nancy and I had a chance to spend a week at the Kwai River Christian Hospital, our old stomping grounds back in the seventies. We had planned the occasion so our arrival would coincide with the hospital Christmas party which indeed it did so we got to have a nice Karen Christmas dinner. About the time the pageant started though we were interrupted by the arrival of a patient from one of the many refugee camps in the area. This didn't bother me too much, though, as these pageants seem to go on forever. Some are good but these infernal amplifiers these days drive me crazy. That was one good thing about when we lived there, no electricity so no amplifiers.
   The patient had been in labor for two days when found by the refugee worker. Dr. Keith took her in and in the process of examining her shook hands with the little critter who didn't have enough sense than to try to come out hand first instead of head first. We then went to the operating room where Dr. Keith extracted the infant and sure enough it was a boy baby causing all the trouble. As I had suspected we hadn't missed much of the pageant by the time we were finished. In the three months or so that Dr. Keith had been there he had already done about eight emergency sections which is quite a few for such a small hospital but it is the only place in the area where they are done.
   Dr. Keith took me on rounds the next morning, then took off for Kanchanaburi with his wife Lois for a much needed rest leaving me to look after things with the good help of Peter, a family practice resident doing a rotation there. The visiting doctors who come to help seem to be a great help as the place has a tendency to get busy at times, well in fact most of the time. It was nice to be back in the place and get the feel of a long past familiar place.
   The thing that pleased both of us was seeing all the faces that we had known when we were there still busy at work in the hospital. Now that is what I call stability when you can leave, be gone for sixteen years and come back to find everybody still in their place. Well, we cannot forget our two Australian Baptist nurses, Josie Falla

and Jan Stretton, who contributed so much in those early days. Josie is back in Kangaroo Kountry and Jan lost her valiant struggle with cancer a few years ago. The original local staff, Ebra, our RN, Olivia the public health worker, Rebecca, our nurse-aid, and Martinee the cleaner-laundry worker were all still serving and happy about it. Then with all the new ones added over the years, what a crew!

The refugee situation there has gotten much worse in the last few years. The Mon refugee camp there has about eight thousand people in it now. I never did find out just how many Karen camps there were nor how many people are in them. They are many scattered up and down the border. One infant was brought in with cerebral malaria while we were there and they had to travel by car about eight hours. When we were there refugees were steadily fleeing the oppressive regime in Burma but in a small manageable stream. There were plenty of places where they could farm so there was no crisis as today. We heard plenty of horrow tales though even in those days about Ne Win's "Road to Socialism" in Burma. Where it has been tried in what country has Socialism not wrecked havoc?

The two wooden salas had been moved to the new location with the hospital and looked exactly as they did when we were there. Both were filled with TB patients about fifteen in all and of course with much of their families so was quite a crowd. Most of them are from the camps. The hospital is doing a vital work just in the TB business.

The hospital is a busy place now and not at all the quiet paced place as when we were there. It was a bit confusing at first, but I got used to it. There was so much going all the time. It had a dynamic atmosphere that became infectious after a while. Every one seemed to have a caring and compassionate attitude.

One of the aspects of the hospital that I have tried to keep up with over the years is the village health ministry. Before we went up to work there Cecil Carder told us to go look it over then come back and write up a proposal for work there. At that time there were no roads, so travel to the hospital was difficult and/or expensive. A person didn't go to the hospital unless he was very sick and by that time he was usually too sick to go. Our emphasis was on village health and preventive medicine.

I caught a bit of flack for being away from the hospital and in the villages so much. Yes, we did have a few unfortunate occurrences while I was away that I may have been able to prevent. The nurses ended up caring for a newborn for six months once because the mother died of postpartum bleeding. That was the wife of Apee, a Muslim who had done a lot of work for the mission over the years. That was tragic and I felt terrible about it and still do.

However the village health program did get off to a smooth running process at last and I didn't have to go on the village trips. Olivia took charge of it and is still in charge. With her team they are doing a tremendous job, and I think that they prevent as many or more diseases as are cured in the hospital. Ten years after the program had been started she told me that she didn't know of a single death in her population of regular under-five clinic attendees. Now that was in an area where the under-five mortality was twenty-five to thirty percent that is one or two children in every family of four or five children would die. Olivia and her team have developed such a reputation that many children graduate from her under-five clinic after five years without missing a single monthly clinic. Some still walk hours to attend with their children at the hospital now that the government has stopped them going to the villages.

That trip to the Kwai Hospital was medicine to our souls. We are glad that we had a little part in the process which has developed so well under the guidance of Dr. Phil and Melba McDaniel.

Sincerely,
J. Freeman

Christian Hospital
Maesariang
31 December 1993

Dear Krista,

When you are out in the jungle and a problem comes along that you don't know how to handle, you just have to do the best with what you have. You have heard that before, and you don't have to be in the jungle either.

There is a good example of that came to me the other day. We were up in the Kwai Hospital, working in place of Dr. Phil where we worked with refugees in the early '80's. We had only been there a day or two when a woman in her thirties was brought in with a gunshot in the upper left abdomen. I looked her over and calculated that the bullet could have gone through the stomach, spleen, colon and a few other things. She had just sold some cows and someone had found out about the sale. Whoever it was decided that they would help themselves to the money.

It was the spleen that I was worried about most since a bleeding spleen is a bad business. It was evening and the boat trip to the hospital in Kanchanaburi would take eight hours or more, and we would have to wait until morning. We had no general anesthesia, so we would have to rely on a spinal for the operation. On top of that, we had no one experienced in spleenectomies, but I had watched a couple.

We calculated the risks and decided to go for it. I looked around and found an anesthesia book to read up on a "high spinal" since the regular spinal would only relax the lower abdomen and the spleen is in the upper. Then I chanced onto a chapter on anesthesia extenders, which I felt would be needed since a spinal anesthesia works for a limited time and a spleen operation can take a long time.

Armed with my newfound knowledge, I told Ebra to start getting the OR ready. We found a unit or two of blood from someone else, so fortunately I didn't have to supply that. After everything was ready, I went out and cranked the generator and was ready to start.

When I walked into the OR, there was Ebra, calmly getting the instruments ready. Ebra never got unglued about anything, and seeing her helped to calm my jitters. Jitters yes, because I'm not much of a surgeon. Down in central Texas they would call me a shade tree surgeon. That was their term for any amateur. But in this case, the poor woman had to take what she could get, and that was me.

The high spinal worked real well, so it wasn't long before I was going after that punctured spleen. Those things are not that easy to get out, especially for newcomers, but out it came and with no damage to the tail of the pancreas as far as I could tell. About that time the spinal started to wear off and muscles began to contract so it was time for the spinal extender. Ebra mixed some xylocaine with saline which I then poured into the belly to numb the peritoneum. That worked, so I looked for other holes. I think the stomach was spared, but there was another hole in the descending colon. Now a good surgeon would have probably whipped up that colon and made a colostomy, but I didn't think there was enough time for that, so I just sewed shut the hole in the front side of the colon. Quickly I looked for other damage, then began to close the wound as she began to lose the anesthesia effect. Just as I was putting in the last stitches, it dawned on me that I had overlooked the hole in the posterior wall of the colon. It was too late to turn back though, as she was now pushing against the wound with muscle contractions. I thought to myself that we would just keep her from eating for a few extra days and maybe that hole would heal by itself.

Several days went by and all seemed to be going well; then her fever began to spike, indicating infection somewhere. Well, I thought there would surely be an abscess around the colon, but no, it turned out that she had empymena. That dirty bullet had come out of the colon and went through the lower part of the lung and set up infection. We put a tube in the chest to drain out the pus, and after a few days things were back to normal or almost. A few days later the patient complained that she had a pain in her back. We turned her over and there was an abscess on her lower left chest. Ebra brought in a scalpel. When we made the incision, out popped a round bullet, with the pus. Then she had to recover from that. By that time I was ready to see the end of that lump of lead.

A couple of days before our month was up and leaving time came, the woman was up and walking around the hospital. Needless to say, I was tired of looking at her, but it was nice to see her get well and go home. Like I said, if you do the best you can with what you have, most of the time things will turn out OK.

Love,
Dad

THE WILD WA

My trip to the Wa began about the middle of the year 1994 as we were leaving Thailand after the year in Maseriang Christian Hospital. It was then that we were told about the Wa by Allan and David Eubank who had already made a trip or two to the Wa for missionary teaching sessions. I was invited to accompany them on the next trip in 1995 with the purpose being to evaluate their medical needs and then develop a village health program for the Wa.

When the British first encountered the Wa tribe in Northern Burma what they found was a rather wild and unruly bunch of tribal people prone to drunkenness and with the nasty habit of taking heads from neighboring villages and tribes. The time for taking of heads was just before planting season, as the heads were believed to ensure a good crop so was a fertility custom. New heads were placed in creches carved from a post and planted alongside the main trail leading to the village where they were left to rot. A visitor to a Wa village would be greeted with an assortment of heads and skulls in various stages of deterioration. The British found out early on that the Wa were especially fond of the fair skinned heads as they would go further in appeasing the spirits. With those habits the tribe was aptly named the Wild Wa. It was that wild nature that led to an argument between the Chinese and the British who both argued that the Wa was on the others territory as neither wanted them to govern. The Wa are located on the China-Burma border area.

Since each village of the Wa took heads it was incumbent on each village to protect themselves from other villagers who wanted a good crop as well. Elaborate defensive fortifications were built around the villages for protection. Mounds, ditches, fences, and strong gates as well as brier bushes were used for safeguarding their own heads. Needless to say the defensive measures involved a lot of time, and all labor was needed for survival in the mountainous and often barren areas of the Wa homeland. Getting enough to feed the family was always a touch and go matter, which may have been another contributing factor to their wild nature.

Their home-made millet beer helped to ease the tensions resulting form trying to protect their own heads while out to get other heads but that added to the problems as it used up scarce grain needed for food. No doubt the Wa were aware that other hill tribes did not subscribe to practice of headhunting. It came to pass that a shaman in one of the villages (Ta Bu Kya Mong) had a dream one night in which it was revealed to him that if his white horse was followed it would lead to a man who had a book that would release them from the head hunting habit.

Having been told of the shaman's dream the villagers were not long in organizing for the expedition in search of the man with the book. On the auspicious day twelve Wa men went out to the edge of their village where the shaman released his white horse. Armed for protection with spears, crossbows and long knives the twelve followed the horse, which ambled in a southerly direction. For days on end the following continued in the southerly direction until the men began to doubt a successful outcome. Finally they decided that the next day they would return home. Morning came but the horse was determined to continue in a southerly direction so the men decided to give him one more day.

By then they were in another tribal area and about dusk they were led into the compound of a newly built house. The white horse walked over and looked down in a hole being dug for a well. William Marcus Young a new missionary of the American Baptists was in the bottom with a helper doing the digging. He looked up and saw the horse and the twelve armed with their spears and inquired as to their mission. When they told of their mission to find a man with a book William climbed out of the hole and admitted that indeed he did have a book. They remained for several days as William taught them from the Bible. They wanted him to return with them to their village but he had come to work with the Lahu tribe so could not accompany them on their return trip, William invited the Wa to send a delegation to learn more of the Gospel which they did. In 1908 the first Wa were baptized.

January the twenty-fifth our little group was on a Thai Airways flight from Chiang Mai to Kunming, China. The group included Allan Eubank, his son David and wife Karen and the great grandson of William Marcus Young, Mark Young and his wife who had recently arrived in Thailand to work with the Wa. We were mixed in with a planeload of Thai tourists on a shopping jaunt to Kunming.

As we flew along I reflected on Allan's story of how the first contact was made with the Wa following the collapse of communism in South East Asia. Sai Pao was one of the leaders of the Wa having been in their army but at the time of our trip supposedly involved in fighting the opium trade. About 40% of the opium grown in South East Asia is produced in the Wa State. Sai Pao was also, as the rumours run, involved in a gambling establishment north of Chiang Mai. Sai Pao on discovering that David was an ex-ranger and special-forces officer invited David to go to the Wa and help them. So here I was on about the third trip into the Wa State with them.

Sai Pao had been involved with a little turf battle with General Lee who was an old Kuomintang officer left in the jungles in the late forties by the fleeing Chang Kai Chek. Men from Sai Pao's faction planted a large quantity of dynamite in General Lee's Chiang Mai back yard and when it was detonated there was substantial damage to Allan and Joan's house, and another missionary's house was destroyed. General Lee survived and decided relocation was the wiser course so moved to the Three Pagoda area just north of our Kwai River Hospital. It was in General Lee's simple bamboo house there that we had our first mobile clinic in that primitive jungle setting. At that time General Lee was involved in wolfram mining in the Karen State.(photo:Gen Lee's elephants) On our village clinic tours we would now and then encounter an elephant pulling a wooden sled or a two-wheeled cart loaded with wolfram ore headed to the Bangkok market. General Lee very graciously made his Three Pagoda home available to us on our visits. Sai Pao was later shot dead probably over a drug dispute.

The main order of business in Kunming was to locate the man who had the Wa New Testaments that were to be picked up and transported into the Wa State. Interestingly it was Sai Pao who had been the contact person in arranging for the Bibles to be printed in China and moved to Kunming for our pickup. Some of the Wa were involved in translating the Old Testament into Wa which I suppose is still an ongoing process. The New Testament translation had been completed in 1933, by the compatriots of William Marcus Young. Rev Joshua who traveled with us in the Wa state was one of the prinsiple translators of the New Testament.

This was my first trip to mainland China but there were many memories from childhood about the exploits of the Kunming based Flying Tigers of General Chennault's little U. S. supported rouge air force as they fought the Japanese in that remote little World War II saga. Those independently recruited pilots flew their P-40 planes painted like tigers as they relentlessly tormented the Japanese army in that area. One evening in Kunming an elderly Chinese gentleman met us and in rather good English introduced himself and then invited up to his apartment. He had been a young man at the time of the Flying Tigers and worked for a tailor who had made many items for the American pilots. He was quite proud of his modest but adequate home and brought out some mementoes of those old days. We could sense his thrill at having someone with which to share those earlier times.

While in Chaing Mai I had lunch with Eugene Morse who with his family had remained isolated in the mountainous Northern Burma with the Lisu tribe during the whole time of World War II. When the U. S. Air Force flew the C-47 cargo planes over "The Hump" from Eastern India to Kunming to re-supply the Tigers, they had to fly over the area where the Morse clan lived. Those are very high and rugged mountains with turbulent weather so claimed many of those planes. The Morse family organized a search and rescue mission to save the crews of those planes. Messages were sent to all the Lisu villages that the men in those planes were their friends and arranged rewards for helping them. Forty years later President Reagan awarded them a medal for their service during that time (The fascinating story of the Morse family has been recorded in the book <u>Out from Hidden Valley</u>).

The building of the Death Railway by the Japanese, which I had become very familiar with was but one of the many other sagas of World War II that occurred in scattered places in Asia. On our most recent visit to the Kwai River Christian Hospital. Olivia took us to see the small Old Folks Home that the church had organized. An elderly Karen man of about ninety was a resident there as he had no family and was alone in the world. He had fought in the jungles with the British against the Japanese during that time. Those jungle battles between the Japanese and the British, with their Karen cohorts was another saga.

Simao was our next destination as we headed southwesterly toward the China-Burma border. From our plane we got a good view of a city of several thousand surrounded by beautiful tree covered hills with rice fields filling all the valleys. The area around Simao seems to be typical of what I had always envisioned of rural China. From Simao we would travel by bus to the city of Lanchang near the border crossing. The six hour drive to Lanchang took us through some very scenic areas with orchards in bloom and terraced rice fields. For an hour or two we paralleled the deep gorged Salween River, which formed the Thai-Burma boundry just west of Maesariang. We would travel on that deep rushing clear water River as we visited Karen refugee camps. That river had an interesting course as it originated in Tibet. As we neared the Burma border the people were dressed more and more in tribal costumes.

Leaving Lanchang about 9:30 in the morning we threaded our way through valleys increasingly more tropical. The morning mist shrouded valleys gave us some breath taking scenic views that helped take our minds off the rough roads in the uncomfortable bus. By the time of our border crossing, which was pleasantly uneventful, the evening had overtaken us and I began to add more clothes as we were approaching five to six thousand feet altitude. At 10:30 PM we arrived at Tao Mei, which was a United Wa Army settlement. It took a while to arrange accommodations for our group, which by this time had increased by the addition of two European journalists who would accompany us, as they were interested in getting the story of the Wa and opium production. By this time we were in the Golden Triangle, the famous opium producing area of Asia. The China-Burma border is sharply demarcated by the different vegetation peculiar to each side. Opium poppies are all along the Burma (Wa State) side and mustard is grown in perfusion on the Chinese side. Though the Chinese do not allow opium cultivation it is reported that most opium and heroin is transported from the Wa state through China.

The night was much spent by the time all of us managed to find a sleeping place but the sleep was peaceful there in the close proximity of the of the commander of the United Wa State Army. However I will have to admit that upon entering the Wa State, where the last incident of head taking was as late as 1970, there was the apprehension that a bit of nostalgia may creep into the scene especially where a group of fair skinned heads were intruding. The American Baptists were responsible for the start of villages without head posts along the entrance paths. The faith and perseverance of the twelve and the white horse had paid off. The American Baptists had also been responsible for the life changing habits of the head hunting Nagas of Eastern India. It was a Christian Naga whom I had seen coming to consult with my friend Jim McKinley in Dacca in 1971. We must give credit to the communists for when they were in control the last vestiges of head hunting were wiped out including the head posts and anything that remained of head hunting.

We were crowded into an old Chinese army jeep as we left Tao Mei toward our final destination. We drove past rather beautiful mountains equal in my opinion to those of Switzerland. Here and there women were out collecting the sap from the base of the poppy blossoms from which opium is made. We drove over an improved dirt road probably made possible by the help of the Chinese stimulated by money from the opium trade. At one place we were introduced to a Chinese colonel or general who was assigned to the Wa Army. At one spot the truck was stopped for repairs and we enjoyed the awesome silence of the area with only the distant clack of bells from free roaming cows. After about six or seven hours of winding mountain roads we arrived at our final destination of Baan Wai.

Bits and pieces of the story of U Saw Lu the central figure of Baan Wai had been told to me and here we came face to face. U Saw Lu had been born into the family of a Wa Christian pastor and consequently grew to be a leader of the Wa. For many years the Wa were divided into the Burmese Socialist faction and the Chinese Communist faction. With the demise of communist influence in the area the Wa developed into an autonomous state. U Saw Lu became the leader of the Burmese Wa with the Burmese attempting to use him to unify the Wa state with the Burmese state government. The Burmese in a ceremony to seal this relationship wanted him to bow down before a Buddhist statue, which was to be televised. He steadfastly refused to bow to a statue upsetting the Burmese to the extent that they placed him in a completely dark dungeon until he relented. Rather than relent he prayed for light while his wife and child were in a separate cell. In the darkness he heard something fall into his cell. Groping around he found a package of candles and matches. With his prayer answered he began to pray for freedom, which was soon granted. He sold his property and moved to the Wa State where he began to publicize the evil dealings of the Burmese government. The government sent soldiers to kill him but they were discovered and disarmed and sent back to Rangoon. Now U Saw Lu was under the auspices of the United Wa Army working to improve the economy of the Wa and to ensure their autonomy. It was his invitation sent through Sai Paa to David Eubanks and the missionaries in Chiang Mai was the genesis of our trip.

Greeting us at Baan Wai were about 35 pastors already gathered for Allan's pastors conference the following day. When we had been showed our quarters the next order of business was to take our turns at the public bath in the corner of the yard. It was made of a fifty gallon barrel kept full with water flowing from a bamboo pipe stuck into the side of the rock cliff. The ice-cold water was enough to eliminate any sluggishness left over from the long ride.

The dinner in U Saw Lu's house was followed by the customary worship service that he directed. The hymn "Draw Me Nearer" was followed by a sermon by Allan then the famous "Candle Ceremony" was performed by U Saw Lu to commemorate his imprisonment and the candles, which were an answer to prayer. U Saw Lu never tired of performing that little ritual at the evening worship time.

The first night it was late to bed and early to rise as I was wakened at 2:30 AM by Thiery, one of the journalists, telling me that his friend Christophe had fallen and had a bad cut on his head. There was a badly bruised forehead with a bleeding laceration, which I managed with a steristrip and pressure dressing. Christophe was having a nightmare in which he was in a truck falling off the mountain road when he fell out of bed. On the way back to my quarters I noticed the brilliant full moon and again it crossed my mind the idea of nostalgia for head hunting possible getting back into the scene.

The next day started with a seven AM service starting the pastor training conference in which Allan and David were seemingly attempt-

A Wa village surrounded by opium fields.

A view of a Wa village with large flowering trees in the background.

ing to pack a year's seminary into two weeks. Four daily sessions were filled with prayer, preaching and teaching as the poorly trained pastors were exhorted to lead their flocks according to New Testament teachings. Allan, sent out by the Christian Church and the most effective evangelist I had known in Thailand, presented daily demonstrations of methods in evangelism. Choirs came and sang sometimes in English with the rendition of "Send the Light" especially memorable. At times they sang traditional tribal hymns much in the manner of the Karen singing of Thailand and thrilling in its beauty and harmony.

The teaching sessions went on all week with Allan and David and at times Mark, doing the teaching. The Wa supplied the music, which was truly inspirational. A quintet presented "On the Jericho Road" in English, which was very professional. Several of the pastors walked a half-day in from China.

The job assigned me was to give a series of medical lectures. In order to prepare for this I launched a quick health survey to pinpoint the more common and serious medical problems. Hearing that a government medical clinic was in the village that became my destination as soon as possible. It was a nice little building but with almost no supplies available to the "Burmese government" supplied female medical worker. The thing that caught my eye immediately was a young man in uniform operating a hand crank generator, which powered a mobile telephone being used by another uniformed man. Those were Burmese soldiers I was told. Immediately I realized that our presence in the Wa State was known by the authorities in Rangoon. We had been led to believe that this area was controlled by the Wa State army and that we had freedom to come and go as this was at least the third trip by the Eubanks. The consequences of our discovery were later revealed. I had a good talk with the medical worker and returned to our compound.

Tuberculosis was the most serious problem but the cure of that disease was beyond the villager's capability in this remote area so I focused on common problems that could be taken care of with the limited means at their disposal. I went about helping them with problem solving approaches to their medical needs. The Wa had their own medical worker who happened to be a Kachin married to a Wa. Roi Jee, it turned out had been in the Moulmein Christian Hospital nursing program the same time as Ebra who was our head nurse on the river Kwai.

The medical teaching sessions with the pastors went on all week with me questioning them about their medical problems and then working to get them to get their minds into the problem-solving path. With the exception of tuberculosis the range of problems that plagued their rural setting were those typical of most rural settings in other places. Diarrheal diseases were prevalent and the cause of many deaths of the younger children. Scabies was endemic and a tormenting problem for children and adults alike. Malaria caused some deaths but not an extensive problem. They had their own cures, which they shared with me and made for interesting dialogue. Animism was still an influence even in the Christian villages, which made the practice of the sacrifice of chickens common being often a drain on a families meager food supply. That practice was on the behalf of a sick person with the sacrifice made to induce the spirits to leave the afflicted one in peace.

Early in the visit I was requested to see a patient in a neighbor village. It was a typical Wa village of closely clustered houses each one with a kitchen garden in the yard. Odd spaces were occupied with white blossoming opium poppies. Each dwelling was equal in size and shape being oblong with thick thatch roofs that came down within three or four feet of the ground. The structure of the house was of unhewn post and beam with a hand sawn wood floor about five feet from the ground. The space under the floor was for keeping animals at night and a work area in the daytime such as milling rice and basket making. We bent down to get under the eve of the thatch and climbed the ladder into the house darkened by the open fire used for cooking and heating. The patient was a girl about twenty years old severely emaciated and barely able to move. We had noticed, under the house, a crude casket recently completed.

There were glowing coals in the dirt fire pit but the light came from the lone 18 inch square thatch roof window which was propped open. It took awhile for our eyes to get accustomed to the semi darkness so as to examine the pitiful patient lying on a floor mat. No furniture is in a Wa house. She had been treated for tuberculosis to no avail. TB requires multi-drug treatment, as resistance is an ongoing problem with that disease. The family gave me a history of their

Inside the Wa house of the TB patient. Her parents are near me.

The reception line on entering the village of Chao Teh.

Wa women in Chao Teh's village.

A Wa woman.

treatment. Even though it was a Christian village about six chickens had been sacrificed in attempts to appease the spirits. Those sacrifices were performed outside the village in order to lure the spirits away from the village. The meat was then made into a stew and eaten by the adults of the village rather than given to the debilitated patent who, desperately needed protein nutrition. Other traditional food proscriptions contributed to the patient's malnutrition. We discussed at length a high protein diet but it seemed to fall on deaf ears. Layers upon layers of darkness practiced for generations are not easily pealed back.

On the way back to our village I began to think of another cause of debilitation and that was HIV so I asked the Wa man with us if it was possible that the girl had come in contact with one of the soldiers and contracted AIDS. "Impossible!" was his reply. Sexual codes of conduct are strictly enforced in most of the Hilltribes and such was the case of the Wa. If anyone is even suspected of immoral conduct the family of the man involved must sacrifice a large pig and the whole village invited to partake of the penalty imposed. From that emphatically answered question I went in another direction by asking why the rice storage buildings were so far from their houses. They were placed apart so that in case of a fire their food supply would not be burned. Having observed no locks on the storage bins I inquired about stealing. "There is no stealing in the Wa State." I was told.

Chao Teh had been the topic of conversation since we arrived, as his village was a primary object of our evangelistic efforts. He was the ruler over about 60 villages that were all non-Christian. Chao Teh was the uncle of John, one of the Wa evangelists that accompanied us to his village. The Gospel had been presented to him some years earlier but since he had four wives at that time he was told that he was not qualified to become Christian. He then developed his own religion, simple as it was, and based largely on spirit worship. It was said that about one hundred villages adopted him as their spiritual leader. So with that many people influenced by him it became a priority of the Christians to seek his conversion and that was the primary goal of our visit to his village.

At Chao Teh's invitation we started out on the five or six hour walk to the village carrying our belongings for the three or four day visit. Horses had been sent out to meet us about half way, which

A chicken sacrifice outside Chao Teh's village.

Preparing curry from the sacrificed chicken.

would carry the older members of the group, Allan and myself included. It was a rather awkward feeling astride that tiny horse but having walked three hours I managed to get used to being carried. About a quarter mile from the village we were met with the greeting party, which consisted of a single file of men, women and children all eager to shake our hands as their greetings. Some of the older men had their homemade ancient spears and others had various kinds of shooting irons. Others had symbols, gongs, and flutes for their musical welcome. Never had I been greeted in such a manner so it was a special sensation.

An evangelistic service was organized for that evening in which, Allan and David presented the Gospel with a lantern-slide program. Following the evening meal we all gathered around in Chao Teh's public room for conversation with the Chief. It being the time of the Chinese New Year there was a constant stream of village chiefs and dignitaries from surrounding villages coming to offer obesience to their chief. Offerings of sticky rice, popcorn and candles were lavished while the chief sat beside his large spirit box with a candle burning in front of it. This same room was were Allan and I slept or tried to sleep as there were large rats scurrying around all night but fortunately there was plenty of popcorn on the dirt floor to satisfy them. That went on each night we were there for there was a constant flow from neighbor villages of those wishing to make offering to the chief.

The village was filled with visitors so the evangelistic services the second day were well attended. We had some private conversations with the chief in which, he admitted that he knew about Christ and that he had contemplated becoming a Christian as several of his children had urged. Other than his several wives he had another problem that being heavy consumption of alcohol and on top of that he was a chain smoker with an attendant whose special duties were to keep his pipes filled. I was asked to examine him, as he was bothered with epigastric distress. My exam revealed a rather healthy 67 year-old man. I ventured to explain to him that heavy doses of alcohol combined with heavy smoking would naturally lead to stomach problems. Cimetidine was in my bag so a bottle of those pills was given to him.

On my morning walk I encountered on the outer edge of the village a man with a freshly killed chicken as he prepared a spirit sacri-

Chao Teh on far right performing ceremony for Chinese New Year.

A Wa man ginning cotton with a primative rollers cotton gin.

fice. Standing at a distance I had for the first time an interesting view of that ritual. A crude survey indicated an under-five mortality rate of about 40 percent which could be drastically reduced with a simple village health program.

One day we walked to a Christian village for a service. It had an interesting history in that during the later time of head hunting it had been brutally attacked and lost about thirty heads. As the village burned the remainder of the villagers fled but eventually they had returned and continued to practice their Christian faith even though suffering such a catastrophe. One of the older men there had on another occasion been kidnapped as a child and held for ransom by headhunters from another village. The ransom was paid so he returned to his family. The journalists in visiting one non-Christian village found several older men who had necklesses with amulets, one for each head he had collected in the old days. There was even one elderly woman who had a neckless with three such amulets.

At one time we sat with Chao Teh as he told about times past. He told about his efforts to eradicate the practice of head hunting. About 40 years ago in his younger days he had searched for the truth and contacted missionaries but they had to leave due to World War II and they never came back He was older now with his many family members and then there was the adulation of the villages that looked to him as their chief so changing to a new religion looked like a distant possibility. Problems however are made to be prayed over so we continued our petitions on the chief's behalf.

Walking though a village one day a man on his porch caught my eye. He was tediously ginning cotton with a primitive roller gin that was slowly doing the job. His was a homemade gin made from rollers and gears carved from wood and fascinating to behold. He had a little pile of cotton with a small bunch of seeds at his feet. That photo that I got that day was one of the favorites of the visit to the Wa State.

The uphill walk back to our compound was rather tiring. The ancient Chinese army truck belonging to U Saw Lu was to pick us up about half way but we passed it broken down along side of the road. That sight caused a bit of apprehension for it was to the conveyance that was to transport us back to the Chinese border. It's two attendants had been busy with that truck all week seeking to make it roadworthy.

On arriving back at Baan Wai we were informed that our tuberculosis patient had died and the funeral had already taken place. That was quite a disappointment for we had worked to make a turnaround in her condition and became a bit emotional about the situation. The next day I went with my interpreter to see the family and visit the grave, which was in the little cemetery at the bottom of the hill below the village. An opium poppy field was adjacent to the cemetery. On the neatly mounded grave were implanted various offerings left by family and friends. We stopped by her house again to take part in another brief memorial service conducted by the Christians.

The last event was the Sunday service attended by a host of Christians from many villages including members from Chinese churches, which innvolved a five or six hour walk. The schedule was filled with various choirs and singing groups who presented their musical talent in a very inspiring manner. Allan preached the sermon about David and Bathsheba with two interpreting one in Burmese and the other in Wa. The size of the crowd that had come walking from all directions made me think it similar to the days of Christ. Only a few years back they were considered the Wild Wa as they lived then in drunkenness and head hunting.

The last day in Baan Wai I reflected on the action packed two weeks amongst the Wa as Allan and David had packed the time with teaching pastors and the evangelistic trip to Chao Teh's villages in efforts to make the most of the time, cost and effort in getting to that remote mountainous area. U Saw Lu had taken us on a tour of his newly planted tea plantation as he detailed for us his plans for economic development for the Wa people. He dreamed of an economy dependent on other than the ubiquitous opium, which was the cash crop used to supplement the rice purchased by the impoverished mountain tribes. Still believing that a new day of opening to the Wa had arrived our group had discussed various ways that we could help them including a medical program, a Bible school and agricultural assistance. We felt a spirit of optimism with our plans and, how they had been received by the U Saw Lu and the pastors. The encounter with the two Burmese soldiers with their hand-cranked radio had faded from my consciousness. Our immediate concern was for the trustworthiness of the antique flat bed truck that was to transport us the twelve-hour drive to the border along a continuous mountain road. At two AM I made my last trip to the single outdoor privy a hundred yards distant from our cold tin roofed shelter. At least there was no line at that time of the morning.

We were all gathered at four AM in U Saw Lu's meeting room for a candlelight breakfast followed by a send away service. Major Adaa, the one in charge of U Saw Lu's detachment of Wa State soldiers, was there to lead his band of ten or twelve recruits in the musical part of the service. Major Adaa was a Catholic from the Lahu tribe who hearing about the ambitions of the Wa volunteered his help. Major Adaa was armed with Catholic medallions around his neck and a 45 U.S. Army service revolver strapped to his hip. His wife and two little children were present with their medallions as they mixed with that band of rebel Baptists. It seemed to me that Major Adaa's primary duty was to teach his disciples English that being one of the important means to bring the Wa into the modern world. I had led his group in several sessions related to medical problem solving where there was no doctor. My theme was the story that Jesus told about the grain of mustard seed and that if we had that much faith there was no limit to what we could achieve. Mustard being plentiful in their gardens seemed appropriate to the occasion.

One of the of the most memorable experiences of my life was the performance that candlelit morning as Major Adaa, armed with his service revolver, leading his little band of Baptists as he played the accordion and they sang in perfect English, "Come and Go With Me to My Fathers House." That was a hymn that I hadn't heard since my childhood days in the little Rockport Baptist Church during which I was studying about Adoniram and Ann Judson in our Royal Ambassador group. These Wa Christians were the spiritual descendents of the Judsons who gave their lives for the people of Burma. He also gave them the first Bible in Burmese. In addition the Judsons were the first foreign missionaries sent by the American church.

A couple other hymns were presented one in English and the other a native hymn all sung with perfect harmony. A devotional and prayer concluded the service and we parted to board the truck before a hint of sunrise. My prayers were then centered on the truck for the thought of a long walk over those mountain roads was a bit daunting. Allan and

Collecting sap from opium plant.

I being the seniors were offered the front seat next to the driver. The remainder of the party including the journalists perched in the back among the baggage and other miscelaneous items. The truck with the assistance of the resident mechanic came to life and in the total darkness we were off to the Chinese border.

As the sun rose over the mist shrouded mountains I was thrilled by the scene of the distant villages some with early Spring orange flowering trees mixed with the thatch roofed houses. When our road was near the mountain-top, we could see range after range of green tree covered mountains. After several sputtering miles the truck came to a halt as our fears rose up. The intermission occurred about mid morning next to a field of poppies in full bloom. Several women smoking their pipes were in the field harvesting opium. With our interpreter I went to get a closer look at the process of collecting the opium. With little three bladed knives the opium pod had been scored the day before and now the white sticky sap that had exuded was being scraped from the pods. Each pod had to be individually handled and scrapped, a very tedious process. After a couple of photos I bargained for a set of tools used to harvest the opium.

The mechanic meanwhile was performing his rites aimed at exorcising the evil spirits from the truck with ultimate success as it again came to life. After the welcome stretch we boarded and were off again toward the border.

On another occasion when the truck had balked David began to relate his experience on his first trip to the Wa. Having received word after the collapse of communism that the Wa wanted help from the missionaries it fell on David the responsibility to investigate the situation. David was a natural born ranger and special-forces type so that was right down his alley. David's route to the Wa border area was similar to the one we had taken. When he arrived he was assigned a Chinese communist escort for his travels there. On one trip David indicated to the escort that he wished to visit a Wa village. One is on that yonder mountain he was told and that he could visit if he wished while the guide waited. So David and his interpreter hiked up the mountain to the village where they were informed that yes it was a Wa village.

As they talked one of the villagers asked if David knew about their village. Neither David nor his Wa interpreter from Thailand knew anything about the village. "We are the first Christian Wa village." they were proudly told. As it turned out one of the men that they met that day was a nephew of one of the twelve men who followed the white horse to encounter William Marcus Young on that day in 1908. So on David's first visit to the Wa he had "stumbled" on the fountainhead of the Wa Christian movement.

By the time that story was over, the truck had been coaxed back to life and, we were on our way again. The trip that day lasted twelve hours with only once encountering another vehicle and that was a two-wheel farm tractor pulling a trailer with several villagers. A great sigh of relief was expressed by our group when, we finally arrived at the border where more reliable transportation was awaiting.

POST SCRIPT

A month or so after returning to the States I received a letter from Allan and David informing me that the very morning of our departure from the Wa State a Burmese army helicopter had landed with the intention of apprehending our group and taking us to Rangoon. It had taken almost two weeks for the army to act on the news sent by the two Burmese soldiers with their hand-crank radio. Allan and David had been given time enough to pack all the teaching and preaching intended into that last trip to the Wa State. Of course we were disappointed that all our development plans had come to nought. The border was not as open as had appeared and the Wa were not in control of their land as had seemed to us. It was also reported that U Saw Lu and his band had been dispersed. So the Wa are still dependent on opium production and at the same time remaining faithful to their Christian heritage.

RETURN TO THE KWAI

There are occasions when God gives us the opportunity to look back into the past and see the results of seeds planted as we struggle to follow His will. These little glimpses into the past give us the encouragement to keep on going. One of these look-backs was the return to the Kwai to participate in the fifty year celebration of the founding of the Kwai River Christian Hospital where we spent the years 1974-77.

Before the letter arrived inviting us to the festivities we had been in contact with Roy and Jill Myers both doctors who had served a term at the hospital before our time there. In their retirement they had become involved again with the operation of the hospital. Roy was especially helpful in the surgery program while Jill worked to upgrade the tuberculosis treatment and control program as there was at the time a thirty bed resident tuberculosis treatment facility at the hospital. A crisis at the hospital developed as the Thai doctor had turned in his resignation and without a licensed doctor the hospital would have to close. At the time of our missionary service Thai medical licenses were issued without a termination date so we were all still licensed to practice medicine in that country. We regretted not seeing the Myers at the celebration but they were making so many trips yearly to the hospital that at that time they were not able to be present. There was an urgent need to have a doctor with a Thai license to fill in the time gaps at the hospital in order to maintain the hospital license.

On my first visit to Bangkok in 1957 there were almost as many klongs (canals) as streets to serve as traffic lanes but in 2010 we found the elevated rapid transit system completed and welcome as it eliminated the traffic jams and noise. Nancy and I with Eiam were picked up at our hotel by an air-conditioned hospital van which deposited us at the hospital in time for supper. When we worked at the hospital it would take us two or three days to make the trip by bus, train, boat, and jungle truck. When we arrived it would take two days to recuperate from the trip.

As we stepped from the van at the hospital a man from an Australian tourist group came over and greeted Nancy and I like long lost friends. Even as he introduced himself as Rob Morgan I still could not remember him. Then he told of how when he first arrived in Thailand with his missionary parents I had discovered him at the Bangkok Christian Guest House and as he seemed at loose ends had invited him to visit us in the jungle. He, being at that time about ten years old, was about the age of my two boys. His parents allowed him to go off into the jungle with a stranger where he stayed with us for about two weeks. After a couple years his parents divorced and returned to Australia. Rob stated that the visit to Sangklaburi was the most memorable event in his childhood. He was at the time of our reunion the pastor of two Methodist churches in Australia.

After breakfast the doctors gathered in the hospital for the brief chapel service which traditionally begins the activities for the day. Dr. Douglas Corporan along with his family started the hospital in 1960 when the place was even more primitive than when we lived there. Dr Philip McDaniel, a third generation Presbyterian medical missionary, followed about two years after we left and served there for about twenty years. Dr. Roy Meyers followed Dr. Corporan and left two years before we arrived. Dr. Sha a Burmese trained Karen doctor led the rounds as he was currently helping in the hospital. The hospital now had thirty beds with the additional thirty bed resident tuberculosis treatment ward.

The building housing the village health program was next on the list of things to see. When we were there an organized village health program was started at the instigation of our Australian Baptist Missionary, Josie Falla, and Olivia our local midwife-public health worker. At the time the whole of Southeast Asia was threatened by a takeover by communism so it was felt that a village health program could continue even if there would be no doctor to replace me. The need for such a program was manifested by an infant mortality rate of fifty percent. That sad situation was caused by malaria, abundance of intestinal parasites, and lack of childhood immunizations, problems which could all be solved with regular visits of a trained public health worker. Over the course of time those problems were largely resolved thus allowing the village health program to morph into a program of case and control focusing on the increasingly problematic HIV epidemic and the increasing number of patients with tuberculosis, many of whom had resistance to multi-drug therapy.

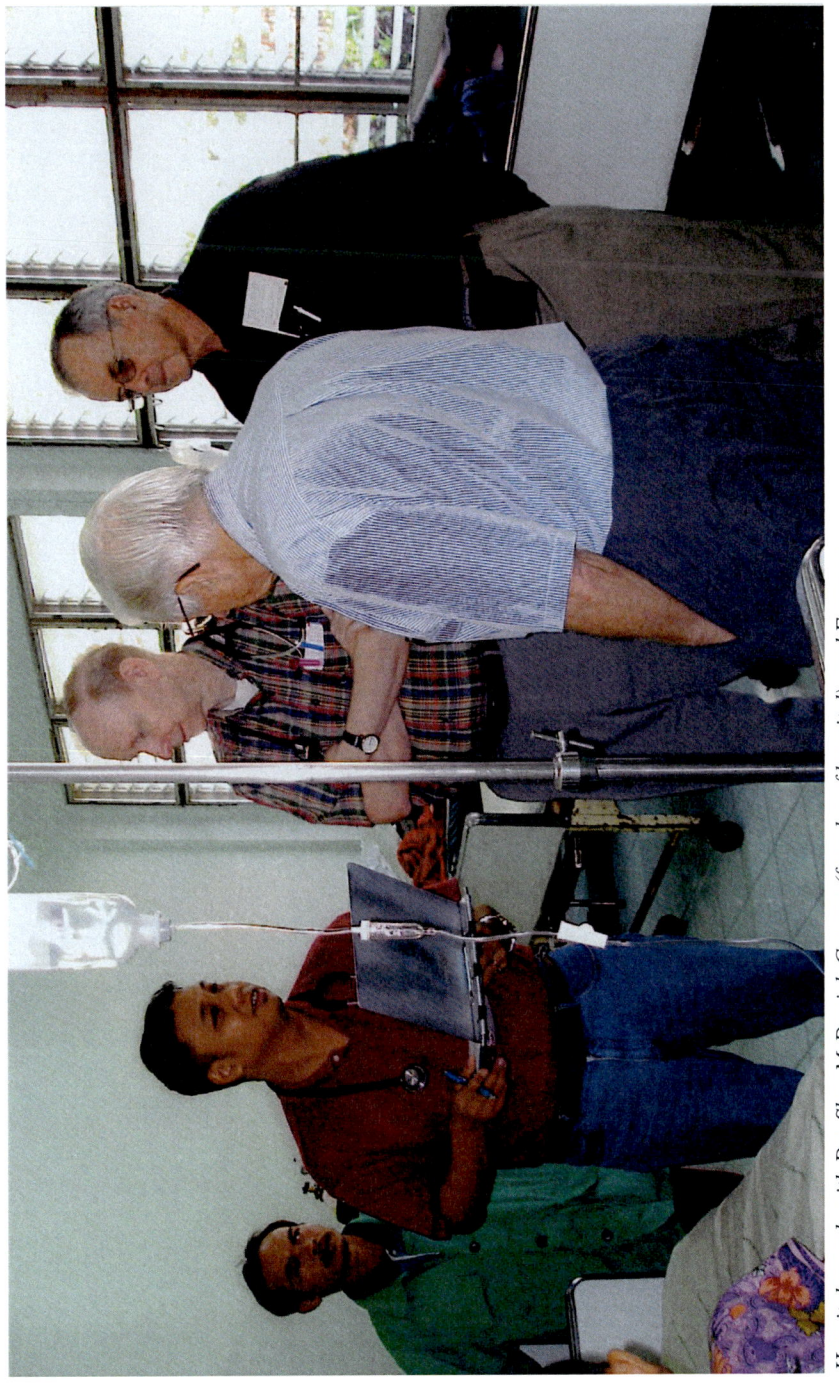

Hospital rounds with Drs Sha, McDaniel, Copran (founder of hospital), and Freeman.

The remoteness and primitive surrounding of the Sangklaburi area always made it difficult in recruiting personnel for both the school and the hospital. It has always been the dream of mission hospitals to eventually have a local person trained as a doctor. Dr. Sakda had been a student in the Christian School when we were there then when Dr. McDaniel arrived he guided him into the field of medicine. He quite successfully filled the needs of the hospital especially with his training in surgery. When Dr. Sakda decided to move to another position it naturally caused a problem as Dr. McDaniel had retired from the field by then. Dr. Sha though well qualified was without a Thai medical license so that limited his usefulness in regard to the official licensing of the hospital. We doctors, along with the hospital administrator, had a meeting to determine which of us would be available on a part time basis to work at the hospital in order to insure the continued operation of the facility in keeping with Thai government requirements. Within a few months the problem was solved as a doctor from another organizations agreed to accept a full time position with the hospital.

The festivities for the occasion included a special service in the church and a fancy dinner with entertainment from the local scene. Life in the sluggish and quiet area that we had inhabited forty years previously had as its only contact with the outside world the shortwave BBC broadcasts on Sunday afternoon. Now there was a satellite TV dish on every house, a cell phone tower in the town with everone equipped with a cell phone. Internet computer service was available and digital cameras were commonly seen. A Seven-eleven store had just opened in the market. Air-conditioned tour buses brought tourists to the area on a daily basis. The jungle had been replaced by groves of rubber trees which were now in production. Fruit orchards and teak forests were common so it was no more the jungle that we had known. I didn't dream that change could be so swift and certain.

One day Olivia took us on a tour to see the current work of the mission. The school with grades one through eight had a nice building for the more than 500 students who attended. When we were there that school was in constant turmoil as one problem after another erupted making it doubtful (in my mind at least) that it would ever be worth the effort. The indomitable missionary Emilie Ballard never gave up and now the school had a stable staff and was turning out students

High School Hostel with railroad wheels which I retrieved from jungle in 1975.

who became teachers for the local area and staff for the hospital. Paw Lulu was trained as a village health worker when we were there and now she is in charge of the Safe House which cares for displaced and troubled adults of whom there are plenty in that area bordering Burma with all its trouble. We were shown a retirement home for those who have no family and an orphanage with about forty children mostly orphaned by the HIV epidemic. Any need that pops up provokes a positive response from the now large group of Christians living in the area.

The Bible School was a new project that caught my attention. The students after getting their training would return to the villages as teachers and workers in the churches. A girl from the Telakon sect was pointed out as the first student from that area that had been off limits when we were there due to communist activity. It was the myth of the Telekon that resulted in the mission being built in the place it is today. In that myth a book was given to them which was lost due to carelessness and the white man was given a book that they safeguarded. The missionaries thought there might be a chance for easy evangelism but in those early days the Telekon rejected the words of the white missionaries. Alan Eubanks was one of the early missionaries to visit the remote Telekon and a person who never gave up in his search to capture the hearts of that tribe for Christ. After the communist days ended Alan resumed his trips to the Telekon and now they have a growing church. It was thrilling to see the first Bible School student from the Telekon which is a branch of the Karen ethnic group.

We had dinner at Olivia's home that evening and what a delight that was. Olivia was one who never tired of going about doing good and I surmised that most of the new projects that we saw that day had the fingerprints of Olivia on them. After dinner she brought out the coat that her father Olive Pa had worn when he spoke before the British Parliament at the time of the turnover of Burma by the British to a newly elected Burmese government. Olive Pa had been the education minister and pled with the British to guarantee some sense of autonomy for the hill tribes who were do disdained by the ethnic Burmese. For his effort Olive Pa was jailed upon his return to Burma where he languished for several years. Finally he managed to escape and fled to Thailand where he found sanctuary.

Olive Pa (his name derived from his eldest daughter Olive so he was called the father of Olive or Olive Pa and his wife was called Olive Mo) was a Telakon who found his way into the service of a timber company early on then went to India for a college education. Olive Mo graduated from a music school in Rangoon so was an accomplished musician. It didn't take long for that very talented pair to be discovered by the missionaries who offered them the job of being hostel parents for the Kwai River Christian Mission Student Hostel. They had been for several years in that position when we arrived at the mission in 1974. By the time we arrived Olive Pa was eighty-five but still alert and with his wife were carrying on a very effective work with the students who came from distant villages where they would not have had the chance for an education. Walking to and from the hospital I was often thrilled to hear the hostel children singing vigorously choruses and hymns being led by Olive Mo as she played the out of tune piano.

It was Olive Pa who with his perfect Queen's English led the first expedition to the Telekon seated on the backs of elephants. As Alan Eubanks tells it Olive Pa insisted on stopping for morning and afternoon tea each of the several days journey. He would have been delighted to see the first Telakon enrolled in the Bible School at Sangklaburi. Often I have wondered at the leading of God as in the case of Olive Pa as he went from being the Minister of Education to the lowly position of hostel parent in that remote jungle setting. That couple who served with such an humble spirit epitomized the theme of the Fifty Year Celebration which was "to the least of these." Walking the pathway of humility has resulted in the wonderful ministries that we observed during those few days at the mission. I don't think Olive Pa and Olive Mo would have had things turn out any differently.

Oliver the brother of Olivia (all ten of the children went by their English names beginning with O) was at the dinner that night along with his son Sonny. Olivia had invited him from his home near Mae Sot to be present when Dr. John and Nancy were to be there. He being second in command of the Karen resistance movement dutifully drove the long distance for the reunion. When shaking hands with Oliver, the hand contraction deformity reminded me of his past bout with leprosy (now cured) and of the times when we would meet at Sangklaburi. Sonny was in the upper grade when we were there and was one of our faithful blood donors. Ebra or Olivia would now and then chase him away from the hospital with, "You just gave blood two days ago and you cannot give again until at least a month has gone by." Generosity came naturally to the family of Olive Pa and Olive Mo. Sonny is now a soldier in the resistance movement and his father's assistant.

Nai Chert was one of the people that I was especially interested in seeing as he was one of the formen in the construction of the bridge which story is told earlier in the book. His daughter was a student in the school when we were there and now has been for many years a teacher there, took us to her house where Nai Chert and his wife were living. We had a nice visit but it was sad to see him in such poor physical health being afflicted with multuple complication of diabetes. His brother Boon Chom was a teacher when we were there and the one who almost single-handedly held the school together. Boon Chom had retired both from teaching and as pastor of one of the churches and was now working with the Bible School. Nai Chert and his younger brother demonstrated both diligence and humility that is remarkable in the contribution to the success of the mission there.

Several villagers who made our life bearable in those earlier days came by for a visit. Waloseng looked after the large hospital garden for the three years we were there. It helped to feed us as well as others. One day he brought in a bullock which was payment by the bear-mauled patient. That bullock became part of a team that for several years was used to pull the Village Health cart on rounds to the villages. Chalong was our house gardner who also came for a visit. There was no market in those days so Chalong helped look after our backyard meat market which included chickens, rabbits, pigs, and goats. He also cared for our little orchard of banana and pineapple plants. Nancy had a happy reunion with Surat who during those three years helped with the house work as Nancy was busy in those days being a school teacher for our four little ones. We were for fortunate to have such dedicated and faithful helpers.

Prapim was a student in our little school when we were there and now is a nurse-aid in the hospital. While we were there her father, a government worker, went with a group of officials north to a village where an election was to take place. On the road they were ambushed by communists and Prapim's father was killed. Naturally that incident created a bit of anxiety in the mission staff and in the village.

Late one afternoon as I was taking a walk through the village a young man stopped me for a talk. When he gave me his name as Komkrit I then remembered him from the school. He was now a teacher in the Christian school. On the way back from the walk I stopped in the hospital and asked the attendent to check my blood pressure. As he was putting on the pressure cuff he looked at me and said, I remember you for you took out my appendix when I was a student.

On our return to Bangkok Nancy, Eiam, and I rode for over an hour on a smoothly paved road through groves of teak and rubber trees some ready for the harvesting of the latex. There was a brief stop at the dam which flooded the upper Kwai valley making the scenic boat trips to the mission impossible now. The loss of that beautiful valley was offset by the electricity that was now available to every village. The night duty nurse at the hospital carried on her duties by candlelight and when surgery was necessary I had to go outside and hand-crank the diesel generator.

On leaving the dam site I reflected on the progress that had come to the Kwai River Valley but the focus of my thoughts were on how the Christians in the area had increased and expanded their ministry to meet the many needs of the area where across the border in Burma there was so much conflict. The little hospital was now the surgical referral center for a Burmese refugee camp of about five thousand. What was currently happening was nothing short of a miracle on the Kwai. <u>Miracle on the River Kwai</u> by Ernest Gordon tells of another miracle during the building of the Death Railroad and it was a wonder to me that God had led Nancy and I to be a part of that struggle in the earlier days. There was a bit of uncertainty in knowing God's will at the time we decided to work in that isolated troubled place but this return to the Kwai cleared away those lingering doubts.

Eiam on the trip back was her usual quiet self. Even she was a miracle on the Kwai for her ofen fatal illness which developed while we were there was cured with never a remission. With Nancy's guidance she had completed her nursing training. She had met us at the airport and arranged transport to Bankok where she had a room prepared for us as she now considered herself rich. On completion of her training Eiam had worked for several years in the Kwai River Christian Hospital but inorder to be close to her aging mother she was now employed in the Bankok Nursing Home Hospital where our first daughter Krista was born while we were in language school.

A brief stop at the real Bridge Over the River Kwai landed us in the misdst of a tourist mecca. From the river shore I looked on the bridge and thought back to the days when my family and I would board a train with a wood burning steam engine, a relic from World War II, which would soon cross, in the early morning mist, that bridge as we made our way up the Kwai River Valley to Sangklaburi. We had barely settled into our home on the Kwai when I answered a late afternoon knock at the door. An elderly gentleman with a perfect British accent inquired of accomodations. Stanly Gimson a survivor of those harrowing days building the Death Railroad had returned to the scene of his and his fellow soldiers misery. He stayed with us for three days as I took him around to some of the remains of the railroad and heard first hand accounts of life in that era. It wasn't but a few months when there was another knock at the door. A trio of British including Patrick Toosey and wife along with Peter Davies had arrived on a fact finding mission. Patrick was the eldest son of Col. Toosey who was portrayed in the movie The Bridge over the River Kwai based on the book The Bridge on the River Kwai by Pierre Boulle. Peter was researching for a book he intended to write in which he would refute the accusations that Col. Toosey (Col. Nicholson in the movie) was a collaborator with the Japanese (Peter Davies later wrote The Man Behind The Bridge, Colonel Toosey and the River Kwai). After a few days with us our knowledge of the Death Railroad was increased and my interest in that saga accelerated. On each trip to Bankok I would go with Nancy to the British Library and check out books about that episode some of which were harrowing stories written by survivors.

The area around Sangklaburi was littered with artifacts from the railroad. Our fence posts as well as others along the trails we traveled and the steps down to the river were made from teak railroad sleepers some still with the spikes as driven in by the prisoners. One of my pastimes was the collection of some of the larger artifacts such as railcar wheels and steamroller wheels. I became aware of the ghosts of the 100,000 men, prisoners and Southeast Asian conscripts, who suffered a disease ridden death building that instrument of war. Those ghosts hovered about as I went about attacking many of the same diseases which plagued the people I was working with. Now those diseases are largely wiped out. On this visit I had not seen one teak fence post to remind me of those ghosts of the past. It has been said that for every sleeper laid down a worker died.

    After arriving back in Bankok we contacted our old friend Dr. Amporn with whom we had worked in the Cambodian refugee camp in the early 80s. She immediately arranged for us to have lunch together the following day. As an infectious disease doctor she had been instrumental in diagnosing the King's near fatal illness in 1983. She and I had worked to describe and publish the mycoplasma pneumonia epidemic in our refugee camp and that experience enabled her to make the correct diagnosis of the King's illness. Since that time she has been a personal physician to the King as well as a personal friend in fact she was to visit the King the same day as we met. Dr. Amporn's ministry to the least had led to that long term relationship with the most beloved king in the history of Thailand.

Seek ye first the kingdom of God and His righteousness

Dr. Amporn with Nancy and John.

John and Nancy are retired and live on the family farm in Bells, Tennessee. Their retirement projects include putting together a rural antique Southern town called Green Frog. That endeavor may be followed on greenfrogtn.org or "Green Frog Village" on Facebook.

Contact the Freemans by email greenfrog412@gmail.com

Made in the USA
San Bernardino, CA
08 July 2015